The Pursuit of Unity and Perfection in History

Other Books of Interest from St. Augustine's Press

The Pursuit of Unity and Perfection in History

KLAUS VONDUNG

ST. AUGUSTINE'S PRESS
South Bend, Indiana

Manufactured in the United States of America.

1 2 3 4 5 6   26 25 24 23 22 21 20

Library of Congress Control Number: 2020947577

∞ The paper used in this publication meets the minimum requirements of the American National Standard for Information Sciences – Permanence of Paper for Printed Materials, ANSI Z39.48-1984.

St. Augustine's Press
www.staugustine.net

Contents

Contents

Preface

The essays in this volume represent major fields of study I was engaged in for more than fifty years. I started out with research on National Socialism; and from the beginning I was interested in the religious traits of the National Socialist ideology and its political manifestations. From my doctoral dissertation[1] until the recent English translation of my book *Paths to Salvation*,[2] I tried to analyze this fascinating and disturbing combination of politics and religion. The essays reprinted here cover some special aspects of this combination.

One of these aspects is the apocalyptic worldview of many National Socialist leaders. The apocalyptic interpretation of the world and history is, of course, not limited to the National Socialist speculation; it is a much broader phenomenon and has a long tradition. Perhaps one can go even so far as to say that—the religious apocalyptic tradition in Judaism and Christianity notwithstanding—secular apocalypticism is the signature of modernity.[3] This would be a statement in opposition to Eric Voegelin's judgment that Gnosticism is "the nature of modernity."[4] The conflict between these two positions will be discussed in several of the essays in this volume.

There are some points of contact of apocalypticism with Hermetic speculations, although Hermeticism is an independent religious and philosophical doctrine. But there are parallels: Apocalypticism as well as Hermeticism

1   *Magie und Manipulation. Ideologischer Kult und politische Religion des Nationalsozialismus*, Göttingen: Vandenhoeck & Ruprecht 1971.
2   *Paths to Salvation: The National Socialist Religion*, South Bend: St. Augustine's Press 2019.
3   Cf. my earlier work, *The Apocalypse in Germany*, Columbia and London: University of Missoury Press 2000.
4   Eric Voegelin, *The New Science of Politics*, Chicago and London: The University of Chicago Press 1952; Phoenix edition 1966, p. 107.

originated in antiquity and they both constituted a tradition that runs until today. They both project a kind of salvation, although with different scope, as the essays in the pertinent chapter show.

The essays in this volume had been presented, before publication, at conferences in the United States and Canada, in Australia and China, in Israel and in European countries.[5] That I could enjoy international scholarly connections had originally been initiated by a postdoc research scholarship, granted by the German Research Foundation. I spent it at Stanford University in 1972 and 1973, supervised by Eric Voegelin. I consequently gained access to the academic community of the English-speaking world. The international connections were further developed because of the interdisciplinary scope of my fields of study, "cultural studies" *avant la lettre*, as it were. The essays in the first chapter of this volume demonstrate the interest in philosophical questions, also articulated in literature, always examined with respect to their political implications. My emphasis on interdisciplinary research is due to the influence of Eric Voegelin with whom I studied in Munich in the 1960s and who was the second reader of my doctoral dissertation. The essays in the last chapter of this volume are to be seen, despite some criticism of Voegelin's work, as a tribute to this great scholar.

Casting a retrospective glance at the essays that were written within a period of four decades, I realized that their diversified themes and subjects notwithstanding there is a subliminal connection between them. It is precisely this that I strive to express in the title of this volume: *The Pursuit of Unity and Perfection in History*. The concepts of "unity" and "perfection" play a role in each and every essay—in some of them directly, in others more indirectly—as goals of intellectual endeavors, as existential ideals, as social or political aims, even as perverse and murderous aberrations (in the case of National Socialism). The essays on Eric Voegelin finally mark a pertinent question: Whether or not the search of order in history might disclose the unity of the history of humankind.

---

5   All, that is, except the review essay on Voegelin's *Order and History*.

Philosophy, Literature, and Politics

The Paradox of Rhetoric
(or: On the Reliability of Written Discourse)[1]

Rhetoric has been connected with politics from its beginning as a particular method or "art" of public speech. It is of fundamental interest in the context of our general theme because of the contrasting roles it has played in this connection and because of the controversial interpretations of these roles. On the one hand, rhetoric has been used and understood as a mediator between philosophical knowledge and political action and thus as a means, as George J. Graham and William C. Havard put it, "to translate *sophia* into political *praxis*."[2] On the other hand, rhetoric has been misused for dubious or bad purposes and therefore has been criticized as a dangerous and contemptible technique of deception and seduction. The full range of possibilities and problems that rhetoric presents was realized during the early stages of its development as a particular *techne*. I intend to concentrate on some major points that those early studies and discussions brought to our attention; it is to be hoped that this will also serve as a supplement to George Graham and William Havard's interpretation of Aristotle's concept of rhetoric.

Although there had been public and, in a sense, political speeches before the development of rhetoric, the origin of a system of rules, which

---

1   Presented at the Annual Conference of the International Seminar for Philosophy and Political Theory on "Politics and its Boundaries: From Sophia to Praxis" at Chateau Montebello, Quebec, 1981.
     First printed in *Sophia and Praxis. The Boundaries of Politics*. Ed. J. M. Porter. Chatham, N. J.: Chatham House Publishers, Inc. 1984.
2   George J. Graham Jr. and William C. Havard Jr., "The Language of the Statesman: Philosophy and Rhetoric in Contemporary Politics," in *Sophia and Praxis. The Boundaries of Politics*, J. M. Porter, ed., Chatham, N.J. 1984, p. 85, 90.

defines how to speak well and successfully in public, is a noteworthy occurrence. It is significant that rhetoric originated in connection with a particular historical event: the overthrow of tyranny in three major Sicilian cities between 471 and 461 B.C. The newly established democratic regimes made it possible, and necessary, to discuss and decide political as well as judicial matters in public. It became important to speak convincingly in court and assembly in order to gain majorities. Hence rhetoric developed as a *techne* that could be taught and learned and whose major concern was the genres of the forensic and political speeches. In 427 B.C., rhetoric was brought from Sicily to Athens by Gorgias of Leontinoi. In Athens the introduction of a democratic regime by

Cleisthenes (509–507 B.C.), together with further political and juridical reforms by Ephialtes and Pericles (462–458 B.C.) had created, as in Sicily, a favorable climate for the use and success of the new *techne*.[3]

In addition to observing the connection between the origin of rhetoric and the establishment of a democratic and lawful political order, we should note a second point that is important for an adequate evaluation of the possibilities and problems of rhetoric; that is, rhetoric made use, probably from the beginning, of the dialectical method developed by the Eleatic philosophers, mainly Parmenides and Zeno.[4] The close connection between rhetoric and dialectic is confirmed by Aristotle, who begins his treatise on *The "Art" of Rhetoric* with the statement: "Rhetoric is a counterpart of dialectic."[5] In order to understand the consequences of the connection between rhetoric and dialectic, it is useful to recall the major changes the dialectical method underwent from the Eleatic philosophers to Aristotle.

Basically, dialectic is a method to discuss contradictory statements. The general scheme of such a discussion can be gathered from Aristotle's *Topics*: The dialectician presents to his opponent a pair of contradictory statements in the form of a question; the opponent decides that one of the statements is correct. Then the dialectician tries to prove the contrary statement by

3   Cf. Cicero, *Brutus* 12.46; Gerd Ueding, *Einführung in die Rhetorik*, Stuttgart 1976, pp. 14–15; Tuttu Tarkiainen, *Die athenische Demokratie*, Zürich 1966, pp. 124–125.
4   Cf. Giorgio Colli, *Die Geburt der Philosophie*, Frankfurt 1981, pp. 68–69.
5   Aristotle, *The Art of Rhetoric*, trans. J. H. Freese, London 1926, 1354A.

questioning the opponent in such a way that his answers form the steps of a deductive argumentation that lead to the final conclusion that the opponent's original decision was wrong.[6]

The usefulness of this method for purpose of public speech is clear. In court as well as in political assembly a decision usually has to be made between the arguments of conflicting positions. Although in public speaking one cannot question an opponent, one can translate the steps and points of the two-sided dialectical argumentation into a one-sided rhetorical argument.

If we want to understand the quarrels about rhetoric, especially the conflicting views of Plato and Aristotle, we must recall that at the time of Zeno and Gorgias dialectic was a highly developed, sophisticated method, indifferent to internal content. Originally the dialectical questioning was not necessarily indifferent to the search of truth;[7] later, as a method of formal reasoning, dialectic tended to evolve into a mere instrument, applicable to the proof of any problem or statement, true or false. Finally, it was the pride of a good dialectician (who was then called a *Sophist*) to be able to prove either one of the contradictory statements in a given dialectical question. Consequently, rhetoric, which made use of this method, could serve as a tool for any purpose.

In Plato's time, dialectic and rhetoric were the twin methods dominating intellectual debate and public speech. It is interesting that Plato adopted and reevaluated dialectic and at the same time rejected and depreciated rhetoric. He rejected rhetoric because it was not an *episteme* but a mere instrument, indifferent to the truth of its content, and therefore open to error and deception. In *Gorgias* he stated: "Thus rhetoric, it seems, is a producer of persuasion for belief, not for instruction in the matters of justice and injustice *(peri to dikaion te kai adikon)*."[8] Of course the method of dialectic Plato found in his time was just as indifferent to "the matter of justice and injustice" as rhetoric; if it was more of an "instruction," it was so only in the sense of formal reasoning.

Plato, however, changed the meaning and status of dialectic fundamentally. He adopted the formal method of argumentation but directed it to

6   Aristotle, *Topics* 104, 108; cf. Colli, *Die Geburt der Philosophie*, pp. 69–71.
7   Cf. Colli, *Die Geburt der Philosophie*, pp. 69, 72.
8   Plato, *Gorgias*, trans. W. R. M. Lamb, London 1925, 455A.

serve truth. In *Gorgias* he redefined the term *techne*: *Techne* can give an account of "the real nature *(physis)* of the things it applies," and it can "tell the cause *(aitia)* of any of them."[9] In the light of this definition rhetoric is not even a *techne* but only a "kind of exercise," a "flattery" to please and deceive the soul.[10] Plato's definition of *techne* shows that his own *techne* of dialectic has become an *episteme* as well—that is, the highest possible *episteme*, which gives an account of the "Good" *(agathon)* as the source *(aitia)* of all being and knowledge.[11] This dialectic as *episteme* and *techne* is the center of Plato's philosophizing and virtually identical with his understanding of "philosophy."

One might ask why Plato chose the method of dialectic as a framework for his *episteme* in the first place? Could he not have chosen rhetoric instead of dialectic, since in either case he still had to develop the epistemological content, which was necessary to focus his method? Or could he not have built up his *episteme* of the *agathon* independently, on a superior level, in order to master both methods, dialectic as well as rhetoric? If we consider that Aristotle reduced dialectic again to an instrumental method, that at the same time he restored rhetoric as a useful "art," that on the other hand he developed separate *epistemai* of metaphysics, analytics, and ethics, these questions are not so far-fetched and useless as they may seem at first sight; perhaps they open the way to additional insights into the problem of rhetoric. Before we follow this train of thought, it will be useful to recall some aspects of Aristotle's view of rhetoric.

George Graham and William Havard have stated that for Aristotle rhetoric, although "neutral as to internal content," is "an art to place in the service of sciences . . . a means in the service of truth," that it "is treated as an important communicative extension of *noesis*," that it "provides a method of transition from *episteme* to *praxis*," and that as such it is "the means of proper political education of the citizen."[12] Without doubt Aristotle restored rhetoric because it can indeed be useful for a proper political education, if guided by proper standards. Probably it was Aristotle's intention to make

9   Ibid., 465A.
10   Ibid., 462B–465E.
11   Cf. Plato, *Republic*, Book. 4.
12   Graham and Havard, "The Language oft he Statesman," op. cit., pp. 80–83.

6

rhetoric a kind of link between *sophia*, the source of the standards, and political *praxis*. Nevertheless, he ran into epistemological difficulties, at least partly caused by his inclination to systematize.

Aristotle defined *sophia* as the combination of *nous*, which enables one to grasp the truth about first principles *(archai)*, and of *episteme*, which enables one to draw conclusions from the *archai*. Thus, *episteme* is concerned with necessary and invariable matters, whereas *techne* and *phronesis* relate to *poiesis* and *praxis* as the domains of contingent matters.[13] *Sophia, nous, episteme, techne,* and *phronesis* together form the dianoetic virtues, the virtues of the rational part of the soul. Although they are connected with each other, since they are ultimately rooted in the divine *nous*, the distinction between invariable and contingent matters makes it difficult to realize the transition from *sophia* or *episteme* to *praxis* when it comes to the question of method. Aristotle carefully distinguished between the methods of *episteme* and those of *phronesis, techne,* and other faculties *(dynameis)* relating to the realm of contingent matters. As to their formal structure, the methods are similar; but as to their validity, they are different. The former, the methods of analytical demonstration, rest on true principles and arrive at true conclusions; the latter, the methods of dialectical and rhetorical argumentation, rest on opinions or probabilities and arrive at conclusions that are only probable. Peter Weber-Schäfer has recently pointed out that by the standards of formal logic, a conclusion pertaining to contingent matters cannot be drawn from true premises, which pertain to the realm of invariable matters.[14] Aristotle himself emphasized the limits of dialectic and rhetoric: "In proportion as anyone endeavors to make of dialectic or rhetoric, not what they are, faculties *(dynameis)*, but sciences *(epistemai)*, to that extent he will, without knowing it, destroy their real nature, in thus altering their character, by crossing over into the domain of sciences, whose subjects are certain definite things, not merely words."[15]

Apart from the epistemological dilemma that dialectic and rhetoric

---

13 Cf. Aristotle, *Nicomachean Ethics,* Book 6.
14 Peter Weber-Schäfer, "Politik und die Kunst der Überzeugung," in *The Philosophy of Order: Festschrift for Eric Voegelin,* P. J. Opitz and G. Sebba, eds., Stuttgart 1981, pp. 345–358.
15 Aristotle, *Rhetoric* 1359B.

cannot serve as methods of *episteme*, there is, in addition, a pedagogical or psychological difficulty that arises from the difference between instruction and persuasion: "In dealing with certain persons, even if we possessed the most accurate scientific knowledge, we should not find it easy to persuade them by the employment of such knowledge. For scientific discourse is concerned with instruction, but in the case of such persons instruction is impossible; our proofs and arguments must rest on generally accepted principles, as we said in the *Topics*, when speaking of converse with the multitude."[16] The rhetorical method of argumentation has to operate with examples instead of deduction, and with *enthymemata*, the rhetorical equivalent of dialectical deduction instead of analytical syllogisms. Since this kind of argumentation cannot prove the truth of its conclusions, errors and deceptions cannot be excluded. Aristotle had to admit the possibility of misuse, but in contrast to Plato, he maintained that rhetoric was nonetheless a "good thing": "If it is argued that one who makes an unfair use of such faculty of speech may do a great deal of harm, this objection applies equally to all good things except virtue, and above all to those things which are most useful, such as strength, health, wealth, generalship; for as these, rightly used, may be of the greatest benefit, so, wrongly used, they may do an equal amount of harm."[17]

But how do we make the right use of rhetoric when there is no methodical guidance through *episteme*? Is it only through goodwill, or even mere chance, that we find the probabilities that come as close to truth as possible in the realm of contingent matters? Yes, as Aristotle explains, the relation between truth and probabilities is much less accidental: "For, in fact, the true and that which resembles it come under the purview of the same faculty, and at the same time men have a sufficient natural capacity for the truth and indeed in most cases attain to it; wherefore one who divines well in regard to the truth will also be able to divine well in regard to probabilities."[18] Although there is no epistemological link between truth and the probabilities of rhetorical argumentation, there is an existential link: the soul of man (of the orator as well as his listeners), which is capable

16   Ibid., 1355A.
17   Ibid., 1355B.
18   Ibid., 1355A.

of actualizing *all* the dianoetic virtues. It is true that rhetoric can be perverted, but virtue cannot, as Aristotle emphasizes. Because of their virtue, the orator and his listeners will be able to link the rhetorical argument with truth.[19]

Thus, Aristotle tried to overcome the ethical indifference of rhetoric by placing it under the reign of virtue. Although Plato had rejected rhetoric, he nonetheless had established the foundation on which Aristotle could construct the philosophical connection between truth and rhetoric. Aristotle's argument that "the true and that which resembles it come under the purview of the same faculty" and that "one who divines well in regard to the truth will also be able to divine well in regard to probabilities" refers directly to Socrates' statement in *Phaedrus* "that the multitude get their notion of probability as the result of a likeness to truth . . . [and] that these likenesses can always be best discovered by one who knows the truth."[20]

Why, then, had Plato not drawn the same conclusion as Aristotle, making use of rhetoric, under these premises, as a means of political education instead of rejecting it? We return to the question raised before. To begin with, Plato's rejection of rhetoric was not so radical as the harsh condemnation in *Gorgias* suggests. In *Phaedrus* we find a more differentiated, though rather confusing, evaluation of rhetoric. On the one hand, Plato repeats his general disapproval of rhetoric, and on the other hand he concedes "that there is nothing shameful in the mere writing of speeches."[21] Obviously, there can be "good writing and bad," so Plato asks: "What is the nature of good writing?"[22] And he replies that "a good and successful discourse presupposes a knowledge in the mind of the speaker of the truth about his subject."[23] It seems as though Plato could come to the same

---

19   Cf. Weber-Schäfer, "Politik und die Kunst der Überzeugung," op. cit., pp. 356–357.
20   Plato, *Phaedrus*, trans. R. Hackforth, Cambridge 1972, 273D.
21   Ibid., 258 D. Plato always and only uses the noun *logos*, or the verb *legein*, for the different types of rhetorical "speech" vs. scientific or dialectical "discourse," written "speech" vs. "living discourse" (i.e., spoken dialectical dialogue); the different English translations depend on the context in which the Greek terms appear.
22   Ibid.
23   Ibid., 259E.

conclusion as Aristotle, derived from the likeness between truth and probability. But this is not quite the case.

The basic subject of any speech, Plato says, not only of the particular genres of forensic ad political speeches, is the soul, because in the soul we actualize the love for the Good, which is the source of all being and knowledge, and because "it is there that the speaker is attempting to implant conviction."[24] Yet the truth about the soul (and with it the truth about all other matters) can be grasped only in the *episteme* of dialectic and by means of "scientific discourse."[25] Does Plato thus revoke his concession that speeches (i.e., written, public, and thus rhetorical speeches) also can be good? Plato's final conclusion seems to be paradoxical: "The conditions to be fulfilled are these: first, you must know the truth about the subject that you *speak or write* about: that is to say, you must be able to isolate it in definition and having so defined it you must next understand how to divide it into kinds, until you reach the limit of division; secondly, you must have a corresponding discernment of the nature of the soul, discover the type of speech appropriate to each nature, and order and arrange your discourse accordingly, addressing a variegated soul in a variegated style that ranges over the whole gamut of tones, and a simple soul in a simple style. All this must be done if you are to become competent, within human limits, as a scientific practitioner of speech, whether you propose to instruct or to persuade."[26]

It is obvious that these conditions cannot be fulfilled in a public speech where one has to address a multitude of people whose different souls one does not know. An additional obstacle is the character of rhetorical speech as a necessarily written genre. (Only in writing can a speech be arranged as perfectly as the "art" of rhetoric demands, and because of its artistic construction, it has to be fixed in writing, otherwise one could not learn and remember it by heart, which is essential for its authentic presentation in court or assembly or elsewhere—Lysias's speech in the beginning of *Phaedrus* exemplifies this.) Writing as such is an obstacle to truth, as Plato contends: "Anyone who leaves behind him a written manual, and likewise anyone who takes it over from him, on the supposition that such writing will provide

24 Ibid., 271A; cf. 246D–248B.
25 Ibid., 270E, 271D–272B.
26 Ibid., 277B.

something reliable and permanent, must be exceedingly simple-minded."[27] And he continues that "a written discourse on any subject necessarily contains a good deal of play, and that no such discourse, whether in verse or prose, deserves to be treated too seriously, but that the best of them were composed only as means of reminding those who know the truth."[28]

Plato's general depreciation of writing aggravates the paradox of the possibility of conveying truth in speech because it includes even his own dialogues, which are fictitious and written literature. If we cannot solve this paradox, we can at least try to get one step further in its interpretation by examining the form of writing in which the paradox is expressed.

The dialogue *Phaedrus* is carefully structured in a succession of ascending steps. It begins with Lysias's speech on love, which serves as an example for a bad speech: It does not define the nature of love and therefore draws wrong conclusions, and it is badly composed. Then follows Socrates' first speech, which is better conceived insofar as it gives a reasonable definition of love, draws more logical conclusions, and is structured more skillfully. But, as a mere antithesis to Lysias's speech, it still clings too much to this bad example and is better only in terms of formal reasoning and composition. Hence, Socrates starts afresh and in a second speech unfolds the true nature of love as a divine force connecting our soul with the true Being. He tells the truth about love, the soul, and the true Being, using a myth, because the telling of a story agrees particularly well with the closed form of the speech and the telling also meets the rhetorical principle of convincing by examples. Yet, for the very reason that the truth was told in a myth, a further step has to be made: When Socrates has finished his second speech he enters into a dialogue with Phaedrus, which not only allows him to reiterate and differentiate in dialectical discourse what he said before but also enables him to discuss the methods one uses to speak about truth, that is, to make the mode of speaking itself the subject of the discourse. And now Socrates comes forth with the surprising statement that everything written, be it speech or discourse, cannot offer "true wisdom, but only its semblance."[29]

Since the preceding sequence of speeches and dialogue represents

---

27 Ibid., 275C.
28 Ibid., 277E–278A.
29 Ibid., 275A.

ascending modes of transmitting truth, it is in the logic of the sequence that Socrates' statement points to a further step. Indeed, Plato takes an ultimate step that reaches beyond the dialogue *Phaedrus* itself, for this dialogue is after all a piece of written literature. The mode of speaking that comes closest to the truth is "the living discourse, the original of which the written discourse may fairly be called a kind of image,"[30] because "clearness and perfection and serious value are only in those spoken discourses that are set forth for the sake of instruction, and are veritably written in the soul of the listener, and have the Just *(dikaion)* and the Beautiful *(kalon)* and the Good *(agathon)* for subjects."[31] The living discourse is by far superior to the written one because only there is the dialectician able to employ the art of dialectic in its full meaning, that is, "to select a soul of the right type, and in it plant and sow his words founded on knowledge, words which can defend both themselves and him who planted them, words which instead of remaining barren contain a seed whence new words grow up in new characters; whereby the seed is vouchsafed immortality, and its possessor the fullest measure of blessedness that man can attain unto."[32]

Now we can answer the question why Plato chose dialectic as the methodical framework of his philosophy: Plato understood the dialectical dialogue not as a mere method of argumentation but as the existential event in which truth unfolds itself in words through the loving interchange of souls that love the truth and jointly search for it.

Nevertheless, we can conclude that the final statements of Plato in *Phaedrus* do not entirely revoke his concession that good rhetorical speech is possible, nor do they invalidate his actual speech about the true nature of love or the dialogue *Phaedrus* itself. Although Plato did not solve the paradox of speaking and writing about truth, he attenuated it, or rather developed an additional view on a different level, by interpreting written speech not as the contradiction but as the "brother" of living discourse,[33] and by placing the different kinds of speeches and dialogue into a sequence in which they represent ascending modes of conveying truth.

30 Ibid., 276A.
31 Ibid., 278A.
32 Ibid., 276E–277A.
33 Ibid., 276A.

With respect to the question of how Plato's final judgment on rhetoric has to be understood, it is noteworthy that the speech of Socrates on the true nature of love forms the structural center of *Phaedrus*. This speech is declared an "exquisite game of the man who is able to play with speech by telling myths about justice and other matters," in contrast to the "vile game" Lysias's speech represented, but also in contrast to the "serious treatment" of truth in the living dialectical discourse.[34] The written dialectical discourse, as we find it in *Phaedrus*, stands between the mythical story and the living discourse; it participates in both: in the truth unfolded in living discourse, but also in the rhetorical character of speech; and it combines, in the very form in which Plato designed his dialogues, the "seriousness" of conversing about truth and the "play" of inventing myths and composing works of literature.[35]

One might conclude that Plato's final judgment on rhetoric was twofold. On the one hand, the hierarchy of speeches and dialogue, which he established, as well as the fact that he wrote speeches himself and used rhetorical elements in his dialogues, allow the conclusion that rhetorical speech can also participate in the truth as the living discourse unfolds, though only as its lesser brother. This conclusion would be similar to Aristotle's view. On the other hand, Plato strictly maintained that for the search and mediation of truth, rhetoric was an inadequate instrument. Thus, the paradox remains, and the task remains for us to make the right use of rhetoric in view of this paradox.

---

34 Ibid., 276E.
35 Cf. the similar paradox of "seriousness" and "play" in *Republic* 545D–546A.

Unity through *Bildung*:
A German Dream of Perfection[1]

"Unity" is something people long for in many ways: they seek to bring their lives, their talents, emotions, beliefs, and actions into a state of existential unity; they strive for the social unification of different classes; they struggle for the political unity of a divided nation; they speculate about the unity of knowledge and faith, reason, and sensuality, matter, and spirit, essence, and existence. In all these cases, and in many more, "unity" is a symbolic equivalent for "perfection." The state of unity is understood as perfect because it dissolves and abolishes differences, discrepancies and contradictions which are experienced as disturbing and deficient.

Despite this general frame of meaning, the symbol "unity" can stand for very different aims and imply a wide variety of contents, as I indicated in my first sentence. In what follows I want to discuss a particular meaning the symbol "unity" took on in Germany in close connection with the symbol *Bildung*. In order to analyze this connection, I have to first explain the German term *Bildung*, especially the meaning applied to it by the philosophy of idealism. On the basis of this clarification, which will also clarify the connection with the symbol "unity," I will trace some major developments of the aspirations hidden behind these concepts. The time-span I have in view stretches from the decades around 1800 to World War I. The justification for dealing mainly with this period will become plausible in the course of my analysis. As the source for my analysis I shall use, apart from the philosophical texts in the beginning, works of literature. That there are material reasons for this choice will also be shown in due course.

1   Presented at the Annual Conference of the International Seminar for Philosophy and Political Theory on "Modern Images of Order and Disorder" at Villa Serbelloni, Bellagio, 1980. First printed in *Independent Journal of Philosophy*, vol. 5/6: Modernity 2 (1988).

I.

Bildung is an extremely complex and particularly "German" concept which makes it impossible to translate into foreign languages. Among the English terms the dictionary lists for *Bildung* are formation, education, constitution, cultivation, culture, personality development, learning, knowledge, good breeding, refinement. *Bildung* indeed can mean all this—and it most often means all this together—but it means still more, and this leads to the core of the problem.

Originally the term *Bildung* meant "form" or "formation" of material phenomena including the bodily appearance of human beings.[2] From here the term's usage was extended to man's "inner personality" so that one can talk about the *Bildung* of a person also with respect to his talents, manners, morals, intellect, character, or soul. *Bildung* can mean a certain stage of personality development as well as the process that leads to it. Since this process can be influenced from outside as well as spring independently from an inborn potential, *Bildung* comprises both planned education and independent self-realization. (This understanding took advantage of the fact that the verb *bilden* can be transitive—*etwas bilden*—as well as reflexive—*sich bilden*.) Transferred from the individual to society and history, *Bildung* can become synonymous with culture and the historical development of culture.

The genesis of this wide scope of figurative meaning goes back to German mysticism of the fourteenth century. The many possibilities of using the terms *bilden* and *Bildung*—transitive/reflexive, process/result, material form/spiritual content—made them suitable for the symbolic articulation

2   Cf. "bilden," "Bildung," *Deutsches Wörterbuch*, Jacob Grimm and Wilhelm Grimm, eds., vol. II, Leipzig 1860, col. 13–15, 22–23; A. Flitner, "Bildung," *Die Religion in Geschichte und Gegenwart*, 3rd ed., vol. I, Tübingen 1956, col. 1277–1281; Rudolf Vierhaus, "Bildung," *Geschichtliche Grundbegriffe*, Otto Brunner, Werner Conze and Reinhart Koselleck, eds., vol. I, Stuttgart 1972, pp. 508–551; Hans Weil, *Die Entstehung des deutschen Bildungsprinzips*, Bonn 1930; Gerhard Kaiser, *Pietismus und Patriotismus im literarischen Deutschland*, Wiesbaden 1961; Franz Rauhut and Ilse Schaarschmidt, *Beträge zur Geschichte des Bildungsbegriffs*, Weinheim 1965; *Die Revolution des Geistes*, Jürgen Gebhardt, ed., München 1968; Walter H. Bruford, *The German Tradition of Self-Cultivation. 'Bildung' from Humboldt to Thomas Mann*, Cambridge 1975.

of very complex matters. And German mysticism took the lead by giving them a new and particular spiritual significance: *bilden* and *Bildung* became symbols for man's advance toward God. The twofold possibilities of usage mentioned above were preserved: the reflexive on the one hand in order to signify God's activity in the movement: *Gott bildet sich in des Menschen Seele*—God reveals himself in man's soul; the transitive on the other hand in order to signify man's activity: *Der Mensch bildet sich Gott ein*—man makes God present in his soul, he 'forms' God in his soul. But also preserved was the double meaning that *Bildung* as the advance toward God signifies the process of this movement as well as its result, i.e., the unification with God in the *unio mystica*. The connection between the symbols *Bildung* and 'unity' which was established here had important consequences for the further development of the concept of *Bildung*.

It would be most interesting and certainly very important to follow this way step by step via Martin Luther, Jakob Böhme, Pietism, Leibniz and Herder, who all helped to modify and gradually change the meaning of these symbols. In the present context I have to confine myself to marking the final breakthrough of a fundamentally new meaning which found its explicit articulation in the philosophy of idealism. Here, as before, the aim of *Bildung* is a state of perfection: unity. But it is no longer unity with God. In the meantime, God had been driven out of the whole of reality. What remained was the immanent "world" and a man who had fallen out of God's hand: the "individual" who found himself confronted with this "world" as an alien reality. At the same time, and in correlation with this development, man had emancipated himself from the old social order and had become an individual also in a social respect. The unity which now is striven for as the aim of *Bildung* is unity with the world in its appearance as nature and society. Through the process of *Bildung*, i.e., through appropriation *(Aneignung)* of the world, the individual seeks to find himself, to realize himself in perfection.

Fichte described the existential dimensions of this process: He defined the Ego as being real only in opposition to a Non-Ego, because the Ego can experience itself only in its restriction by a Non-Ego. The restriction, however, can be felt only insofar as the Ego "impinges" upon the Non-Ego, "attacks" its resistance. Thus the Ego becomes real, i.e., realizes itself, *bildet sich*, in a continuous process of appropriating the Non-Ego, i.e., the world.[3] In a way similar to Fichte, Wilhelm von Humboldt saw the *Bildung* of the individual as "the connecting of our Ego with the world" by which the individual gains "perfect unity."[4]

Hegel outlined the universal and historical dimension of the process of *Bildung*: "The task," he says in the introduction to the *Phänomenologie des Geistes*, "of leading the individual from his *ungebildete* standpoint to knowledge has to be defined in its general meaning, and the general individual, the independent spirit, must be viewed in its *Bildung*."[5] The independent spirit for its part achieves knowledge by passing through "the stages of *Bildung* of the general spirit."[6] And the general spirit forms itself, *bildet sich*, in the course of world history by appropriating the world it is confronted with in successive dialectical steps until it is unified and reconciled with itself.[7]

The connection between the aims of individual and universal unity, which in Hegel's complicated argument is almost obscured, is established more clearly in Humboldt's words. At first he brings the aims of individual and universal *Bildung* close to each other by using in both cases the symbol "the Whole" *(das Ganze)* for the state of unity and perfection: "The true purpose of man is the highest and most proportional *Bildung* of his powers to a Whole."[8] On the universal scale the task is "to accomplish the *Ausbildung* of humanity as a Whole."[9] Then he draws the conclusion: "I feel that I am driven to a state of unity. . . . I find it absurd to call this unity God, because this would mean throwing unity out of oneself unnecessarily. . . . Unity is humanity, and humanity is nothing else

3   Johann Gottlieb Fichte, *Das System der Sittenlehre. Ausgewählte Werke in sechs Bänden*, Fritz Medicus, ed., vol. II, Darmstadt 1962, pp. 485–487.
4   Wilhelm von Humboldt, "Theorie der Bildung des Menschen," *Werke in fünf Bänden*, vol. I, Darmstadt 1960, pp. 235–237.
5   Georg Wilhelm Friedrich Hegel, *Phänomenologie des Geistes*, J. Hoffmeister, ed., 6th edition, Hamburg 1952, p. 26.
6   Ibid., p. 27.
7   G. W. F. Hegel, *Grundlinien der Philosophie des Rechts*, Georg Lasson, ed., Leipzig 1911, § 358.
8   W. v. Humboldt, *Ideen zu einem Versuch, Die Gränzen der Wirksamkeit des Staats zu bestimmen. Werke*, vol. I, p. 64.
9   W. v. Humboldt, "Theorie der Bildung des Menschen," *Werke*, vol. I, p. 234.

than I myself."[10] The triple identification of "unity," "humanity" and "I myself," together with the refusal to accept God as the realization of unity, reveals the "drive" to unity as the aspiration to become a God of the immanent world, i.e., a perfect being, who is unified with himself in perfection insofar and because he is unified with the world he has absorbed. Clemens Menze's summary of Humboldt's concept—"In his *Bildung* man deifies himself."[11]—grasps the core of the new meaning which *Bildung* has assumed in many minds by the end of the eighteenth century, although not everyone put it in such precise terms as Friedrich Schlegel: "To become God, to be a human being, *sich bilden*, are notions that have the very same meaning."[12]

II.

There are two reasons why I now turn to an analysis of literature. The first reason is given by the sources. In Germany we have a particular species of novel which originated in the late eighteenth century, inspired by the new concept of *Bildung*, and which flourished throughout the nineteenth century. The concept of *Bildung* determined the form as well as the structure and content of these novels so strongly that a special term was coined for this literary species: *Bildungsroman*. Wilhelm Dilthey defined the general structure of a *Bildungsroman* as the story of a young man who enters life in the happy mood of dawn, who seeks friendship and love, has to struggle with the realities of life, grows to maturity after various experiences, finally finds himself and reaches fulfillment as a harmoniously developed personality.[13] It can be mentioned in passing that Hegel's *Phänomenologie des Geistes* can be viewed as a philosophical *Bildungsroman* in which a "hero," the "world spirit," struggles with the world he is confronted with and

10 *Wilhelm von Humboldts Briefe an Karl Gustav von Brinkamnn*, Albert Leitzmann, ed., Leipzig 1939, p. 155.
11 Clemens Menze, *Wilhelm von Humboldts Lehre und Bild vom Menschen*, Ratingen 1965, p. 127; cf. Manfred Henningsen, "Wilhelm von Humboldt," *Die Revolution des Geistes*, pp. 131–153.
12 Friedrich Schlegel, "Athenäums-Fragmente," *Schriften zur Literatur*, Wolfdietrich Rasch, ed., München 1972, p. 54.
13 Wilhelm Dilthey, *Das Erlebnis und die Dichtung*, Leipzig 1906, p. 327.

realizes himself *(bildet sich)* by appropriating it.[14] There is, however, a considerable difference between the philosophical concept and a novel, and this difference marks the second reason for my turning to literary sources.

A novel, if it aspires to be good, cannot speculate about *Bildung* and unity in general terms and abstract notions ("deification through *Bildung*"—what does that mean in a concrete sense?). It has to represent the process and results of *Bildung* in a concrete person and in the course of a story. Because of that, literature reveals the existential dimensions of the concept of *Bildung* much better than philosophical speculation, and, what is even more important, it reveals the practical problems of the concept which a story about people and their concrete doings cannot conceal so easily. To be sure, the *Bildungsroman* tends toward the same aim of *Bildung* as in the concept's philosophical manifestations: godlike unity and harmony of the individual with himself and the world. In Goethe's novel *Wilhelm Meisters Lehrjahre* (1795/96), we find the proclamation that man should be a "God of the earth"[15] (although its meaning is not unambiguous there). But literature (again: if it is good) does not speculate but visualizes reality and represents experiences. And we have no experience of a man who became God. The dilemma between the aspiration for perfect *Bildung* and the opposing forces of reality which become effective in the literary presentation of the process of *Bildung*, led to different solutions in the various *Bildungsromane*. This is what makes this genre so interesting for the analysis of *Bildung*.

The paradigm of the German *Bildungsroman*, Goethe's *Wilhelm Meisters Lehrjahre*, provides an excellent example of this dilemma. The hero of the novel, Wilhelm, develops his personality in the course of his conflicts and struggles with the world. He makes an advance toward a state of perfection, but this state is not visualized. Schiller's judgment was correct: "He refuses to give us the direct satisfaction that we demand, and he promises a higher and higher satisfaction, but we have to postpone this into the

14 Cf. Jürgen Jacobs, *Wilhelm Meister und seine Brüder. Untersuchungen zum deutschen Bildungsroman*, München 1972, pp. 100–101.
15 Johann Wolfgang Goethe, *Wilhelm Meisters Lehrjahre. Goethes Werke* ('Hamburger Ausgabe'), Erich Trunz, ed., vol. VII, 6th edition, Hamburg 1965, p. 71, cf. P. 82.

distant future."[16] Considering Schiller's own tendency toward philosophical speculation, this judgment sounds rather critical. As a matter of fact, many interpreters found a certain weakness in this lack of absolute fulfillment, if not even an element of resignation.[17] My own opinion is different. I think Goethe was conscious of the problem the individual encounters if he tries to deify himself. He saved his novel from derailment and kept it in a delicate balance. The pivot of this balance was the renunciation of the central aspiration of the concept of *Bildung*, the decision, as Camus called it, "to refuse to be a god."[18] Ultimately Wilhelm owes his maturity not to his own activities of self-realization. "Basically," Goethe remarked to Eckermann, "the entire novel attempts to say no more than this: that despite all his foolishness and confusion, man, guided by a hand from above, can achieve happiness in the end."[19] And in a discussion with Boisserée, Goethe sharply condemned the "madness and rage of attempting to reduce everything to the single individual and to be a God of one's own right."[20] Instead of deifying himself, Wilhelm accepts the *conditio humana*, and this means: integration into a world and society which are not experienced as absolutely alien and hostile. This can be criticized as resigned and passive only if the self-deified individual is the criterion for judgment. I want to stress that integration into the world and society does not necessarily lead to passivity. For Wilhelm it means action indeed, although not in the sense of appropriation or conquest. At the end of the novel the aim of *Bildung* is defined as "being active in a dignified way," "without wanting to dominate."[21]

In opposition to Goethe's *Bildungsroman*, Novalis presented quite different a solution in his novel *Heinrich von Ofterdingen* (1799). He criticized in Goethe the fact that Wilhelm Meister is made to adjust himself to

16 Letter to Goethe, November 28, 1796, *Der Briefwechsel zwischen Schiller und Goethe*, Hans Gerhard Graef and Albert Leitzmann, eds., Leipzig 1912, vol. I, p. 266.

17 Cf. Jacobs, *Wilhelm Meister und seine Brüder*, p. 80.

18 Albert Camus, *The Rebel. An Essay on Man in Revolt*, translated by Anthony Bower, New York 1956, p. 306.

19 Johann Peter Eckermann, *Gespräche mit Goethe in den letzten Jahren seines Lebens*, Otto Harnack, ed., Berlin n. d., vol. I, p. 119 (January 18, 1825).

20 *Sulpiz Boisserée*, M. Boisserée, ed., Stuttgart 1862, vol. I, August 5, 1815.

21 *Goethes Werke*, vol. VII, p. 608.

reality.[22] Novalis, on his part, adhered to the ultimate aim of *Bildung*: "All *Bildung* leads to something which can only be called freedom, certainly not meant to denote a mere name, but to designate the creative principle of all being. This freedom is mastery. The master exercises free power according to his intention. . . ."[23] However, Novalis could not visualize this aim in a story about the development of a realistic person in everyday life, since obviously God-like mastery cannot be achieved in ordinary reality. He transferred his story into the legendary scenery of the Middle Ages, which was supposed (the novel is fragmentary) to gradually change into a second reality of dreams and fairy tales.[24] The aim of unity and perfection, which again implied appropriation and domination of the world, was to be achieved through the magic of poetry.

Novalis' novel represents one of the two extreme possibilities of falling out of the delicate balance which Goethe had tried to establish between the aspiration for perfect *Bildung* and the opposing forces of reality: If the attempt is made to visualize the state of perfection, the connection with reality is lost. The result is, at best, a fairy-tale of paradise, or at worst, if the poetic abilities are weaker than in Novalis' case, bloodless abstraction. The other extreme results from the experience that self-deification must fail: If this experience cannot be endured, then the world, and with it the individual, is hurled back into alienation and meaninglessness, ending in nihilistic despair. (An example for this possibility will be shown later on.) Between these extremes we find all sorts of variations and compromises. In what follows I want to interpret some of these variations as they were represented in the course of the nineteenth century. Because of the peculiar tension between *Bildung* and reality, above all material and social reality, it will be interesting to view the different representations of the striving after unity and perfection with special regard to a particular aspect: Goethe and Novalis had shown, each in his own way, that the question of whether or

22 Novalis, *Schriften. Die Werke Friedrich von Hardenbergs*, vol. III: *Das philosophische Werk II*, Richard Samuel, ed., 2nd. Edition, Stuttgart 1968, pp. 638–639, 646–647.
23 Novalis, *Heinrich von Ofterdingen*, Wolfgang Frühwald, ed., Stuttgart 1978, pp. 173–174.
24 Cf. "Paralipomena zum Heinrich von Ofterdingen" and "Tiecks Bericht über die Fortsetzung," ibid., pp. 179 seq. and 207 seq.

not one should try to dominate reality, and how this could be brought about, becomes a central issue of *Bildung* when the process and results of *Bildung* have to be visualized in a work of literature. This problem remained constant as long as such literary attempts were made. Therefore, it will be of special interest to investigate how different authors solved this problem under the changing circumstances of material and social reality.

III.

During the nineteenth century, in particular during its second half, German society underwent a radical process of change which also affected the concept of *Bildung* and its realization. Especially the failure of the revolution of 1848 had far-reaching effects. The attempts of the middle class to gain political power in proportion to its social and economic rise were finally repelled. Subsequently the middle class made its peace with the 'old powers' and confined itself to everyday business or inner values *(Innerlichkeit)*. At the same time the industrial revolution began to alter the social structure of Germany radically. Apart from the development of a strong working class, the most important result of industrialization was the disintegration of the middle class, which had previously been a relatively homogeneous class (known as the middle-class of property and *Bildung*—again a symbol of unity). An industrial *bourgeoisie* arose which ascended to the higher ranks of society. Craftsmen and tradesmen whose professions became obsolete descended into the proletariat. A "new middle class" of engineers and clerks developed. The old intellectual class *(Bildungsbürgertum)* was left behind, uneasily wavering between the fronts.

The concept of *Bildung* of this class became more and more rigid. In a society which had a greater demand for scientific and technical education than for Latin and Greek, *Bildung* degenerated to a mere veneer. Now the price had to be paid for the fact that the German universities and *Gymnasium* had followed too exclusively the neo-humanistic concept of Humboldt with its overemphasis on "inner *Bildung*,"[25] on "inner improvement and refinement" of man,[26] and on the perfection of his "inner

25 W. v. Humboldt, *Werke*, vol. I, p. 238.
26 Ibid., p. 235.

existence."[27] Consequently these institutions of higher education had slighted the 'trivial' sides of reality, although one could have learned from Goethe not to neglect "realism"—science and even technology—for the sake of idealism. Thus, not only the social unity of the intellectual class, but also the unity of *Bildung* was lost.

Literature played a special role in this development. On the one hand it was, with its authors and their products, part of this development, and on the other hand it tried to depict and analyze the development. This was done in different ways; the following examples may serve as illustrations.

No better representative of the time after the revolution of 1848 can be imagined than Gustav Freytag. He felt himself to be totally in tune with his time, prepared for all activities and professions of *Bildung*—as a scholar, journalist, poet, and even politician. His novel *Soll und Haben* (1855) became a bestseller which remained an inalienable part of *bourgeois* bookcases almost up to the present day.

Soll und Haben is a social novel, but it is also a *Bildungsroman*. In comparison with *Wilhelm Meister*, however, the aims of *Bildung* are cut back. The world in which the process of *Bildung* takes place has become smaller, it is the world of middle class business. Freytag characterized the dominant theme of the novel with a motto of his friend Julian Schmidt: "The novel should seek the German people where they can be found at their efficiency, i.e., at their business."[28] In this smaller world, however, undejected self-confidence and optimistic belief in the future prevails. The hero of the novel is Anton Wohlfart, an apprentice in a merchant's house. His process of *Bildung* leads him through the risks and hazards of business life to the aim of becoming an independent merchant and proprietor. It is true that this aim is adorned with a garland of virtues which is supposed to crown the hero's prosaic materialistic success and unite it with *Bildung* of his character, but these virtues are only secondary: industry, diligence, efficiency, and, at the most, honesty.

Soll und Haben represents a kind of *Bildung* which discards all idealistic dreams, aesthetic fantasies, and elevations of the soul; contemporaries defined this kind of *Bildung* as "realistic." The critic Karl Gutzkow detected

27 Ibid., p. 60.
28 Gustav Freytag, *Soll und Haben*, Leipzig 1855, motto.

(and criticized) the retreat from the greater realm of *Bildung*: "These 'modern' men Herr Freytag has invented are intended to be nothing but real, i.e., just what they are. They are not supposed to have extra beliefs, they are only to live for business and commerce, wheel-barrows and haggle. The consequence of this brilliant rationalism and lack of any message is an infinite sobriety which pervades all these inventions, a deplorable emptiness of the mind, the poorest fertilization of the heart, the poorest fertilization of fantasy."[29] What Gutzkow did not detect and appreciate was the attempt to actualize a new, indeed realistic, and timely unity of *Bildung* on a smaller basis: Freytag was no loner striving for the self-realization of man through absorption of the whole of reality, but for the self-realization of the *bourgeois* through appropriation, i.e., domination of the material and social world. This meant self-realization through labor and with an ethos of labor which included the practical virtues fitting for a middle class God.

And yet this unity was already lost when it was conceived. The figure of the "merchant-prince" as representative of the middle class had already been superseded by the new leaders of industry and banking. And with the rise of the latter the unity of the old middle class business world was also destroyed. It is true, the prophet of the new times, Karl Marx, adopted the *bourgeois* ideal of self-realization through labor, but the new class of the proletariat was to realize it against the *bourgeoisie* and in a more global sense.

The constraint in Freytag's attempt to realize unity at least in a smaller realm was observed by Adalbert Stifter immediately after the publication of the novel. "Everything is just fabricated and made up," he remarked, "therefore nothing is worked out and organic."[30] However Stifter found himself in no less precarious a situation when he set out to actualize a quite different ideal of *Bildung* in his novel *Der Nachsommer*, which came out two years after Freytag's *Soll und Haben*.

It has been debated as to whether or not *Der Nachsommer* is a *Bildungsroman* at all, for it lacks one of the most important characteristics: the hero's process of *Bildung* through crises, confusions and errors. Heinrich

---

29 Karl Gutzkow, "Ein neuer Roman" (1854/55), *Liberale Energie*, Peter Demetz, ed., Frankfurt a. M. 1974, p. 337.

30 Letter to Gustav Heckenast, February 7, 1856, *Theorie und Technik des Romans im 19. Jahrhundert*, Hartmut Steinecke, ed., Tübingen 1970, p. 54.

Drendorf, the hero of the novel, develops step by step without negative influences or obstructions from the outside and without inner temptations, only indirectly guided by his mentor Risach. Apart from this mainly literary criterion another point is even more substantial for the problem of *Bildung* in *Der Nachsommer*: if the aim of *Bildung* is the self-realization of the autonomous individual through appropriation of the immanent world, i.e., self-deification, the aspiration for such an aim must have been anathema for the believing Christian Stifter. But this was precisely the dilemma: he was not only a Christian, but also a *Bildungsbürger* and a child of his time. Herder and Humboldt had had great influence upon his education, Goethe was his literary paragon. The events of the time were not without influence upon his work; his experience of the revolution of 1848 and its consequences form the background of *Der Nachsommer*, although it plays no visible role in the novel. "Probably," he confessed, "I have written the novel because of the meanness which in general and with few exceptions rules the political conditions in the world, moral life, and poetry. I wanted to set a great simple moral force against the miserable degeneracy."[31]

For Stifter *Bildung* essentially is the realization of this force in unison with the highest and general law which he called the "law of justice and morality,"[32] i.e., God's law. The aim of *Bildung* is a "pure humanity"[33] which has arrived at the "universal" and the "whole."[34] These symbols of unity must not be confused with those of immanent unity between the individual and the world; he identified the "whole" with the "divine."[35] In the novel, however, religious elements remain in the background, and this fact signifies the dilemma I have just mentioned: the novel sets out to represent a kind of *Bildung* whose aim ultimately again would be unity with God, but this *Bildung* is realized, at least partly, in activities through which the emancipated individual usually strives for his autonomous self-realization: exploration of nature, sciences, art, literature. Moreover, Stifter tries to visualize

31 Adalbert Stifter, *Sämmtliche Werke*, August Sauer et alii, eds., vol. XIX: *Briefwechsel III*, 2nd edition, Prague 1929, p. 93.
32 A. Stifter, *Bunte Steine* (preface), Leipzig n. d., p. 13.
33 A. Stifter, *Sämmtliche Werke*, vol. XIX, pp. 94–95.
34 A. Stifter, *Bunte Steine*, p. 11, cf. A. Stifter, *Der Nachsommer*, Max Stefl, ed., Darmstadt 1963, pp. 13, 382–383.
35 A. Stifter, *Sämmtliche Werke*, vol. XIX, p. 199.

this *Bildung* in a literary species which was activated and characterized mainly by the immanent type of *Bildung*.

The dilemma had various consequences for Stifter's novel. The first and perhaps most important is the principle that the way of unity cannot be pursued in the attitude of a conqueror, but, as Risach says, "in reverence for the things, as they are themselves," in an attitude in which one does not look for one's own "profit" but "for that which the things demand for themselves and which is in accord with their essence."[36] Consequently, Heinrich's process of *Bildung* is an almost contemplative opening up of himself to this essence of things. In comparison with Wilhelm Meister, who has been criticized as passive, Heinrich Drendorf certainly is the most passive hero imaginable. Even imagination, which plays a dominant role for the heroes of other *Bildungsromane*, is excluded here. If one wants to grasp the "truth" of things, Risach remarks, one must not cherish "delusions" or "imaginations."[37]

The second consequence of the dilemma is the insignificance of art as a creative activity. Stifter wrote about this to Louise von Eichendorff: "In *Der Nachsommer* art is represented as an ornament of life, not as its aim."[38] The contemplative and restorative attitude toward art which manifests itself in Heinrich's drawing beautiful furniture and Risach's restoring old objects of art is often criticized as unproductive and regressive.[39] Indeed the way is short from here to a *bourgeois* culture which has the atmosphere of a museum where the treasures of Bildung are merely locked up and catalogued.

But this is not quite the case in Stifter. The word "restoration" has a negative ring from the first for many people, although only the concrete content of that which is restored enables an adequate judgment. The restoration of our old towns and cities is a good example. If destruction of the old becomes unbearable, and the new that replaces it cannot satisfy, we rejoice about the restoration of conditions that allow a more human life.

---

36 A. Stifter, *Der Nachsommer*, p. 701.
37 Ibid., p. 119, cf. P. 46.
38 Ibid., p. 851 (quoted from Max Stefl's epilogue).
39 Cf. Max Rychner, "Stifters Nachsommer," *Welt im Wort*, Zürich 1949, p. 165; Fritz Martini, *Deutsche Literatur im bürgerlichen Realismus 1848–1898*, 3rd edition, Stuttgart 1974, p. 523.

Probably this holds true not only for architecture. At any rate, Stifter experienced the destructions of his time, the "miserable degeneracy" and the "decay" of the world as so radical that first of all he wanted to restore what he considered as fundamental: "pure humanity." Thus, the third consequence was that the world of labor, society, and politics remained outside of his novel. In the state in which this world presented itself to him he could neither incorporate it into his concept of *Bildung*, nor did he want to conquer it. Since Stifter, unlike Goethe, no longer experienced the world and society as generally ordered and meaningful, he took his hero out of this environment, in accordance with the principle, formulated by Heinrich's father, that "man primarily does not live for the sake of society, but for his own sake." However, the principle was followed by the hope: "If everyone lives for his own sake in the best way, he does it also for the sake of society."[40]

The novel *Der Nachsommer* sets out to be a paradigm. It has the paradigmatic character of some legends of saints in which the saint achieves bliss and salvation without struggle and sin, solely through the devotion to God. *Der Nachsommer* appears like a *Bildungsroman* only on the surface; it should be called instead a 'legend of a middle class saint'. This is not meant pejoratively but serves to express the paradox of Stifter's search for unity.

If Stifter was unhappy because of the wickedness and degeneracy of the world, he still had his belief in God. Gottfried Keller, another important novelist of the time, lost even this under the influence of Feuerbach. Thus, the hero of his *Bildungsroman, Der grüne Heinrich* (1854–55), now definitely is a 'modern' individual. Without guidance by a "hand from above" or a mentor like Risach, he has to fight his way through a hostile world which again and again throws him back on his incongruous self. His attempt to realize himself through conquest of the world takes the form of his aspiration to become an artist. He wants to achieve unity through imagination; he tries to create a world "which existed only in my mind."[41] The artistic aspiration relates, as a symbolic image, to the general problem of human *Bildung*. Because not only as an artist, but also in his personality,

---

40   A. Stifter, *Der Nachsommer*, p.14.
41   Gottfried Keller, *Der grüne Heinrich. Gesammelte Werke in vier Bänden*, vol. II, Leipzig n. d., p. 227.

Heinrich has a tendency to swindle. As a boy he takes to thieving in order to indulge in childish confidence tricks. Later on, he abandons himself to an overenthusiastic and quite unreal love. And finally, he lets his mother perish while he pursues his selfish dreams.

The artist's attempt to exploit and appropriate the world "for selfish purposes"[42] is defeated by reality. Furthermore, Heinrich must experience feelings of guilt as a result of this attempt. In the first version of the novel, he does not find a way out of this situation. He breaks down and dies within a few days. The novel ends in despair. And yet there is another solution that Keller's own experiences during his life made conceivable and which was realized in the second version of the novel. The acceptance of guilt is the basis for forgoing conquering the world. Heinrich attains "devoted love for everything being and existing, a love which respects the right and signifi-cance of every single thing."[43] He attains that openness toward reality which was achieved also by Goethe's and Stifter's heroes. Despite Feuerbach, Keller had preserved, or opened up again, a "basis for life" *(Lebensgrund)*,[44] and this symbol without doubt refers to nothing else than to the meaningful whole of reality which is more comprehensive than the 'world'. On the other hand this basis for life was no longer certain enough to keep life, as in Goethe, in a harmonious balance and lead it to a "happy end." The ex-perience that unity cannot be established led Keller into a "deep funda-mental sadness" *(tiefe Grundtraue)*[45] which underlies also the second version of the novel. Although the confidence in the basis for life rules out despair in this version, full happiness can no longer be attained, only the reduced happiness of a "short evening glow."[46]

With the second version of *Der grüne Heinrich* (1879–80), we ap-proach the end of the century. The ruptures in *bourgeois* society as well as in the world of *Bildung* have become so deep that a reconciliation which goes beyond Keller's is no longer conceivable. Keller's solution has been

42 Ibid., p. 348.
43 Ibid.
44 Ibid., p. 349.
45 Letter to Wilhelm Petersen, April 21, 1881, quoted from Hermann Boeschen-stein, *Gottfried Keller*, Stuttgart 1969, p. 17.
46 G. Keller, *Der grüne Heinrich*, p. 780.

called resigned,[47] and this view can be affirmed, if absolute self-realization is the criterion for judgment. However, in the light of the perils and problems Keller encountered in his world, one should instead stress the courage with which Keller faced this world and his own existential problems. In any case, a *Bildungsroman* in the classical sense did not seem to be possible any more after *Der grüne Heinrich*. Among the numerous novels of Fontane, for instance, there is not a single *Bildungsroman*, although he did write about the problem of *Bildung* and unity, especially in his novel *Frau Jenny Treibel* (1892).

The plot of this novel centers on the attempt of Corinna Schmidt, the daughter of a *Gymnasium* professor, to marry into the family of a leading industrialist, *Kommerzienrat* Treibel. Although she succeeds in making a conquest of Treibel's son Leopold, her plan is thwarted by Mrs. Jenny Treibel, the industrialist's wife, whom Fontane designated as the "type of a bourgeoise."[48] A process of *Bildung* does not take place in this novel, if one leaves out of account that Corinna finally realizes not only that she cannot succeed but also that her aspirations were wrong. *Bildung* appears no longer as a possibility of the individual to realize himself autonomously but is presented in its social significance. The plot of the novel is determined by the broken social unity of the middle class. The gap between the industrial *bourgeoisie* and the intellectual class with its lower social prestige has become so wide that Corinna's attempt to unify mind and money must fail. "Socially it may work for a while," remarks her father, "but not for a whole lifetime. It might be possible to marry into a duke's family, but not into a *bourgeois* family."[49]

The unity between property and *Bildung* which Mrs. Treibel represents is only for show. She always talks about the true happiness of the "higher" values but throws these values immediately overboard when Corinna takes her by her word and tries to marry into her house with no other dowry than intelligence and charm. The agility with which the *bourgeoise* Jenny Treibel usurps the air of *Bildung* and uses it as a mere ornament for her life

---

47 Cf. Jacobs, *Wilhelm Meister und seine Brüder*, p. 184.
48 Theodor Fontane, *Frau Jenny Treibel. Sämtliche Werke*, Walter Keitel and Helmuth Nürnberger, eds., vol. IV, München 1963, p. 368.
49 Ibid., p. 465.

of pleasure shows something else, though: not only the social unity of property and *Bildung* has been lost, but the realm of *Bildung* itself has lost its vigor and imperial aspirations for unity. Only with difficulty does the realm of *Bildung* continue to defend itself behind a wall of auto-suggestive self-assurance. A colleague of Schmidt gives a revealing reason for the necessity "to believe in ourselves and our cause": "It is not necessary to believe in what is right, but that one believes at all, that's the important thing."[50] The most devastating verdict on such an attitude is formulated by Treibel, who is depicted by Fontane not without sympathy: "He who believes in a way and a cause is always a *poveretto*, and if the cause he believes in is he himself, he is a public danger and a candidate for the madhouse."[51]

Nevertheless, this novel too speaks about "perfection,"[52] a perfection which in Schmidt's eyes his daughter Corinna is striving after. It is a special kind of perfection, however, a perfection in the style of the Schmidt family "which never becomes oppressive because one's ironic attitude toward oneself always puts a question mark behind the perfection."[53] Irony toward oneself is a human quality which balances the inescapable tension between the insight that unity cannot be reached and the attempt to strive for self-realization all the same. Schmidt calls the standpoint of irony toward oneself the "highest conceivable standpoint."[54]

Looking back, we realize that humor and irony had the same significance in *Wilhelm Meister* and *Der grüne Heinrich*, and that it is not by accident that the optimistic and self-confident *Soll und Haben*, as well as the saintly and earnest *Nachsommer*, lack this mode of expression almost entirely. The attitude of humor and irony toward oneself is only possible if reality is generally accepted, including its negative sides. One must not be a "touchy fellow or a spoil-sport,"[55] as Schmidt says and shows; one must give others their due even if they are not in the right. No doubt, this is a standpoint which is difficult to carry out. The less one finds meaning in

50   Ibid., p. 352.
51   Ibid., p. 309.
52   Ibid., p. 364.
53   Ibid., pp. 364–365.
54   Ibid., p. 347.
55   Ibid., p. 369.

reality, the more difficult this becomes. It can easily happen then that irony turns to satire; Fontane's novel come close to that several times. The pregnant words of the epilogue come from Professor Schmidt: "Money is nonsense, scholarship is nonsense, everything is nonsense." The bitter seriousness hidden in these words regain the balance of self-irony only by his adding: "Professor is too," and of course due to the fact that he is not entirely sober when he says this.[56]

IV.

The cue had been given though. "Everything is nonsense" became the most disturbing experience of the times to come. The technological and anonymous mass-society, which dawned by the end of the century, put higher and higher obstacles in the way of individual self-realization according to the idealistic concept of *Bildung*. Fontane had demonstrated how unworldly and ridiculous, but also dangerous, the aspiration for dominating reality through *Bildung*—be it spiritually or socially—had turned out to be. Although the fallacies and dangerous implications of the concept of *Bildung* were obvious from the first, when it was formulated by philosophers of idealism, it is owing to literature that the concrete consequences of these implications were shown by visualizing persons who tried to realize *Bildung*. Whether the attempt was made to gain unity and perfection in and through poetry, as in Novalis' case, or to dominate reality by reducing it to the smaller realm of *bourgeois* business-life, as in Freytag, or to reconcile the activities of *Bildung* with Christian belief, as in Stifter, in all these cases the unbridgeable gap between the ultimate aim of *Bildung* and reality became obvious. At best a precarious state of balance was reached, which in Keller's case, for instance, had to be struggled for in the teeth of despair. It is interesting that in the beginning as well as at the end of the history of *Bildung* we find particular attempts to achieve balance, in *Wilhelm Meisters Lehrjahre* and in *Frau Jenny Treibel*, although this balance was achieved in very different ways. Goethe was still able to establish a harmonious relation to reality which he could accept as meaningful, without having to create meaning by dominating reality, whereas Fontane, one century later, found neither

56   Ibid., pp. 477–478.

harmony in the world and society of his time, nor any hope of bridging the ruptures and discrepancies he experienced, least of all through *Bildung*. The only possibility to obviate and endure the imminence of meaninglessness was in the attitude of irony toward the world and himself, which enabled him to criticize the nonsense of the world without falling into despair, and which at the same time preserved him from taking some of the nonsense seriously himself.

Two decades later even this balance was lost. World War I, which brought the era of the old middle class to an end, induced German intellectuals to try in a last desperate effort to force unity and to dominate reality through *Bildung*. The Hegelian philosopher Adolf Lasson, for instance, proclaimed the unifying and dominating power of *Bildung* by declaring even the German engine of war to be an emanation of the German spirit.[57] The historian Otto von Gierke demonstrated the unity of the nation by listing the achievements of its different classes and professions; the fact that his role of praise is led by civil servants, professors, artists, and engineers (in this order) discloses the continuing ambition for intellectual domination.[58] The pastor Karl König believed that the war would unify religion and technology and thus also recreate social unity rooted in the spirit.[59] The nonsense that resulted from such interpretations was so tremendous that irony became helpless and even satire had to give it up, as Karl Kraus observed.[60] The history of the ambitious concept of *Bildung* had come to an inglorious end: by its most extreme consequences, it was led into absurdity.[61]

57 Adolf Lasson, "Deutsche Art und Deutsche Bildung," in *Deutsche Reden in schwerer Zeit, gehalten von den Professoren an der Universität Berlin*, vol. I, Berlin 1915, pp. 122–123, 138–139.

58 Otto v. Gierke, "Krieg und Kultur," *Deutsche Reden in schwerer Zeit*, p. 85.

59 Karl König, *Neue Kriegspredigten*, Jena 1914, pp. 25, 38.

60 Karl Kraus, *Die letzten Tage der Menschheit* (preface), München 1957, p. 9.

61 If the term still plays a role in today's discussions of education, either this fact or the term's traditional meaning has been forgotten.

German Nationalism and the Concept of *Bildung*[1]

In the series of public lectures which professors at the University of Berlin gave after the outbreak of World War I under the title *Deutsche Reden in schwerer Zeit*, Adolf Lasson, Professor of Philosophy, spoke about *Deutsche Art und deutsche Bildung*. Lasson defined the German character and German unity as being rooted in the German *Geist* and represented by German *Bildung*. In his eyes *Geist* and *Bildung* formed the fundamental substance of the German nation to such an extent that he considered all manifestations of the nation's life and all of its accomplishments to be ultimately emanations of the two.[2] Even the engine of war, which was now set in motion against other nations, he saw in this way: "Our army and navy are also a spiritual power *(Geistesmacht)*. In Germany, military *Bildung* is an inseparable ingredient of all general *Bildung*, not an additional kind."[3] But Lasson regarded *Bildung* not only as the constituent and special quality of the German nation, but also as proof of Germany's superiority over other nations and as justification for the mission which she was now to execute with military force. "Our superiority is indubitable," he exclaimed to his audience; and addressing the other nations: "Why don't you first imitate our elementary school teacher, our *Gymnasium* teacher, our university professor!"[4]

---

1   Presented at the International Conference of the Humanities Research Centre on "Romantic Nationalism in Western Europe," Australian National University, Canberra, 1980.
      First printed in *Romantic Nationalism in Europe*, J. C. Eade. Ed. Canberra, Australian National University, Humanities Research Centre, 1983.
2   Adolf Lasson, "Deutsche Art und deutsche Bildung" (25.9.1914), in *Deutsche Reden in schwerer Zeit, gehalten von den Professoren an der Universität Berlin*, vol. I, Berlin 1915, pp. 111, 122, 123, 138, 139.
3   Ibid., p. 142.
4   Ibid., p. 140.

The loose connection between nationalism and the concept of *Bildung*, which Lasson demonstrated, was commonplace among German professors, poets, and pastors in World War I. This connection has been established at the time when German nationalism as apolitical doctrine was born—during the time of Germany's occupation by Napoleon and the Wars of Liberation. In his memoirs, Ernst Moritz Arndt records that in the year 1813 he met Fichte in Berlin placing spears and swords in front of his house for himself and his adolescent son, remarking: "Only over my dead body shall the enemy enter the city."[5] Arndt, who was familiar with Fichte's philosophy, knew how to interpret this event. "In his patriotism," he commented, "Fichte apparently found the bridge over which he could cross from his ideal Ego to the Non-Ego."[6] Since the progression of the Fichtean Ego to the Non-Ego, i.e., the world, is a process of *Bildung* (more about this presently), this event revealed in Arndt's eyes the nexus between the concept of *Bildung* and nationalism.

Before I give a more detailed analysis of the connection between German nationalism and the concept of *Bildung*, I must make a few remarks about the latter.[7] *Bildung* is an extremely complex and particularly "German" concept, which makes it impossible to translate. Originally the concept had nothing to do either with nationalism as a political doctrine or with politics. Basically, the term means the "form" or "formation" of material phenomena, including the bodily appearance of human beings. From here the term's usage was extended to man's "inner personality," so that one

5   Ernst Moritz Arndt, "Erinnerungen aus dem äußeren Leben," *Ernst Moritz Arndts Sämmtliche Werke*, vol. I, Leipzig n. d., p. 184.
6   Ibid.
7   See "bilden," "Bildung," in *Deutsches Wörterbuch*, Jakob Grimm and Wilhelm Grimm, eds., vol. II, Leipzig 1860, col. 13–15, 22–23; A. Flitner, "Bildung," *Die Religion in Geschichte und Gegenwart*, vol. I, 3rd edition, Tübingen 1956, col. 1277–1281; Rudolf Vierhaus, "Bildung," *Geschichtliche Grundbegriffe*, Otto Brunner, Werner Conze, Reinhart Koselleck, eds., vol. I, Stuttgart 1972, pp. 508–551; Hans Weil, *Die Entstehung des deutschen Bildungsprinzips*, Bonn 1930; Gerhard Kaiser, *Pietismus und Patriotismus im literarischen Deutschland*, Wiesbaden 1961; Franz Rauhut and Ilse Schaarschmid, *Beiträge zur Geschichte des Bildungsbegriffs*, Weinheim 1965; *Die Revolution des Geistes*, Jürgen Gebhardt, ed., München 1968; Walter H. Bruford, *The German Tradition of Self-Cultivation: 'Bildung' from Humboldt to Thomas Mann*, Cambridge 1975.

can talk about the *Bildung* of a person also with respect to his talents, manners, morals, intellect, character, or soul. *Bildung* can mean a certain stage of personality development, as well as the process that leads to it. Since this process can be influenced from outside, as well as independently springing from an inborn potential, *Bildung* comprises both planned education and independent self-realization. Transferred from the individual to society and history, *Bildung* can become synonymous with culture and the historical development of culture.

The genesis of this wide scope of figurative meanings goes back to German mysticism of the fourteenth century, which gave the term a particular spiritual significance. It became the symbol for man's advance toward God. Here too *Bildung* signified a process as well as the result of this process, i.e., the unification with God in the *unio mystica*. The connection between the symbols *Bildung* and "unity" which was established here had important consequences for the future development of the concept.

The spiritual notion of *Bildung* changed its content gradually in the following centuries, finding a new and explicit formulation toward the end of the eighteenth century. Here, as before, the aim of *Bildung* is a state of unity. But it is no longer unity with God. God had been driven out of reality; what remained was the immanent 'world' and a man who had fallen away from God: the 'individual' who found himself confronted with this 'world' as an alien reality. At the same time, and in correlation with this development, man had emancipated himself from the old order of society and had become an individual also in social terms. The unity which now is striven for as the aim of *Bildung* is unity with the world as nature and society. Through the process of *Bildung*, i.e., through appropriation *(Aneignung)* of the world, the individual seeks to find himself, to perfect himself.

The process of *Bildung* was represented in fiction by the *Bildungsroman*, a genre particular to German literature which sprang up in the late eighteenth century; philosophically the new concept of *Bildung* found its distinct articulation in the systems of Idealism. Fichte described the existential dimensions of this process. He defined the Ego as being real only in opposition to a Non-Ego because the Ego can experience itself only in its restriction by a Non-Ego. The restriction, however, can be felt only insofar as the Ego "impinges" upon the Non-Ego, "attacks" its resistance. Thus, the Ego becomes real, i.e., realizes itself, *bildet sich*, in a continuous process of appropriating the Non-Ego, i.e., the world.[8]

Hegel outlined the universal and historical dimensions of the process of *Bildung*. "The task," he says in the introduction to the *Phänomenologie des Geistes*, "of leading the individual from his *ungebildete* standpoint to knowledge had to be defined in its general meaning; and the general individual, the independent spirit, had to be viewed in its *Bildung*.[9] The independent spirit, for its part, achieves knowledge by passing through "the stages of *Bildung* of the general sprit."[10] And the general spirit forms itself, *bildet sich*, in the course of world history by appropriating the world it is confronted with in successive dialectical steps, until it is unified and reconciled with itself "as the objective truth and freedom which are revealed within self-consciousness and subjectivity."[11] This last quotation indicates that despite Hegel's raising of *Bildung* to a universal process, it is rooted still in the existential sphere. Alexandre Kojève and Eric Voegelin have shown in detail that the self-consciousness within which the absolute spirit reveals itself is the self-consciousness of Hegel himself.[12]

At this point we can turn to the connection between the concept of *Bildung* and nationalism. In my attempt to answer the questions as to how this connection was formed, what the basis of its development was, and what consequences it had, I will deal (1) with the structural parallels between the two concepts, which fostered their combination; (2) with their similar or common content as meeting points; and (3) with the historical development of this connection.

(1) The most significant structural parallel between the two concepts is given by the internal tension they both show between individualism and

8   Johann Gottlieb Fichte, *Das System der Sittenlehre. Ausgewählte Werke in sechs Bänden*, Fritz Medicus, ed., vol. II, Darmstadt 1962, pp. 485–487.

9   Georg Wilhelm Friedrich Hegel, *Phänomenologie des Geistes*, J. Hoffmeister, ed., 6th edition, Hamburg 1952, p. 26.

10 Ibid., p. 27.

11 G. W. F. Hegel, *Grundlinien der Philosophie des Rechts*, Georg Lasson, ed., Leipzig 1911, p. 358.

12 Alexandre Kojève, *Introduction à la lecture de Hegel. Leçons sur la Phénoménologie de l'Esprit*, Paris 1947; Eric Voegelin, "On Hegel: A Study in Sorcery," *Studium Generale*, 24 (1971), pp. 335–368.

universalism. As far as *Bildung* is concerned, this tension is apparent in Fichte as well as in Hegel. Wilhelm von Humboldt dealt with this tension in his *Theorie der Bildung des Menschen* in a similar way to Fichte; he saw the *Bildung* of the individual as "as the connecting of our Ego with the world" by which the individual becomes "free and independent" and gains "perfect unity."[13] Clemens Menze has shown that this endeavour has to be understood as a process of self-realization which is to lead the individual to God-like existential perfection: "In his *Bildung* man deifies himself."[14] As a God of the immanent world, however, the individual in his state of perfection has to incorporate spiritually the unity of himself with the world he has absorbed. Hence Humboldt concluded: "I feel that I am driven to a state of unity. . . . I find it absurd to call this unity God, because this would mean to throw unity out of oneself without necessity. . . . Unity is humanity, and humanity is nothing else than I myself."[15]

We find the same ambivalence between individualism and universalism in the political doctrines of nationalism formed in France and the Unites States. Students of nationalism have shown that the idea of the individual who is invested with inalienable natural rights was an essential formative element in the development of nationalism as a political doctrine.[16] The nation for its part, as a union of such individuals, can also be viewed as an individual body which represents these rights. But these rights, freedom, equality, self-government, pursuit of happiness, etc., embody a political humanism which claims to be a universal standard beyond the political order of the individual nation.

13 Wilhelm von Humboldt, "Theorie der Bildung des Menschen," *Werke in fünf Bänden*, vol. I, Darmstadt 1960, pp. 235 seq.

14 Clemens Menze, *Wilhelm von* Humboldts Lehre und Bild vom Menschen, Ratingen 1965, p. 127; cf. Manfred Henningsen, "Wilhelm von Humboldt," Die Revolution des Geistes, pp. 131–153.

15 *Wilhelm von Humboldts Briefe an Karl Gustav von Brinkmann*, Albert Leitzmann, ed., Leipzig 1939, p. 155.

16 Among the numerous studies on nationalism, cf. especially Kenneth R. Minogue, *Nationalism*, London 1967; Elie Kedourie, *Nationalism*, London 1969; Christian Graf von Krockow, *Nationalismus als deutsches Problem*, München 1970; Theodor Schieder, "Typologie und Erscheinungsformen des National-staats in Europa," *Nationalismus*, Heinrich August Winkler, ed., Königstein 1978.

The second structural parallel lies in the *dynamic* character of the two concepts. The process of *Bildung* as a dynamic movement is clearly demonstrated by Fichte's Ego permanently impinging upon and appropriating the Non-Ego. As Fichte remarked: "The *gebildete* man can never be idle nor ever take rest."[17]

The dynamism of nationalism results from the paradigmatic character of its political doctrine, which calls for its continuous realization within the nation and, by virtue of its universal claim, invites other nations to join in these endeavours.

The third parallel extends the second one: it is a tendency to unlimited expansion which can turn into aggression and conquest. If the world the individual wants to appropriate in his *Bildung* is conceived as hostile, the Ego must "attack" it, as Fichte says, and must conquer and dominate it spiritually by incorporating it in a "system," as Hegel does.

The same mechanism can be found in the national "mission": If a nation knows that it represents universal human and political standards, it might happen that it "helps" less developed nations to realize these standards by conquering them.

(2) Let me now proceed to the elements which the two concepts have in common or which resemble one another. There are two major ideas at the center of both concepts: unity and freedom.

Bildung can be viewed, first, as indicated before, as a process which leads to existential unity. In Humboldt's words: "The true purpose of man is the highest and most proportional *Bildung* of his powers to a Whole."[18] This can be achieved by "the nexus of our Ego with the world."[19] *Bildung* as the means of realizing the true nature of man can be viewed, secondly, on the larger scale of the human race—as the means "to accomplish the *Ausbildung* of humanity as a Whole" (Humboldt),[20] i.e., as the instrument to establish humanity in the sense of a unity of mankind, unified by virtue

17 J. G. Fichte, *Grundzüge des gegenwärtigen Zeitalters, Ausgewählte Werke*, vol. IV, p. 541.
18 W. von Humboldt, "Ideen zu einem Versuch, die Gränzen der Wirksamkeit des Staats zu bestimmen," *Werke*, vol. I, p. 64.
19 W. von Humboldt, "Theorie der Bildung des Menschen," *Werke*, vol. I, p. 236.
20 Ibid., p. 234.

of its fully developed humanism. Between the individual and the universal unity we can find, thirdly, the idea of unity as an intermediate: *Bildung* as a process of creating unity within the cultural framework of a nation, based on the common language. Only the community of all nations would then establish the unity of mankind. With this idea the concepts of *Bildung* and nationalism historically intersect. More about this later.

It is hardly necessary to enlarge upon the fact that unity is of course also a central idea of nationalism. Politically (in the sense of French or American nationalism), the unity of the nation is founded on the equal rights of its members and their common will to realize these rights, and it is represented by a government which guarantees these rights. Unity of language as well as cultural, ethnical, and geographical unity can be considered as additional factors.

Nationalism as a political doctrine can also imply the idea of universal unity, as we have seen. This unity, however, cannot be reached by combining the political systems of the different nations, but only when all nations recognize the absolute standard *one* nation represents.

The idea of freedom has such a close connection with the idea of unity in both concepts that one can say they mutually determine each other. *Bildung* in its individual dimension was described by Humboldt as a process of mind "to become free and independent within itself."[21] Hegel defined the *Bildung* of the general spirit in its universal historical meaning as a "movement of liberation."[22] This is logical because the process of unification between the Ego and the world means the abolition of the restrictions which the world imposes on the Ego. Hence unity, as the aim of *Bildung*, is identical with "objective freedom,"[23] as Hegel calls it, or with becoming God, as Friedrich Schlegel put it more bluntly.[24]

Freedom and its synonyms self-determination and self-realization play an equally important role in nationalism, again in correlation with the idea

---

21 Ibid., p. 235.
22 G. W. F. Hegel, *Grundlinien der Philosophie des Rechts*, p. 352.
23 Ibid., p. 358.
24 "To become God, to be a human being, *sich bilden*, are notions that have the very same meaning." Friedrich Schlegel, "Athenäums-Fragmente," *Schriften zur Literatur*, Wolfdietrich Rasch, ed., München 1972, p. 54.

of unity. Politically, unity is based upon the natural rights of individuals, among which freedom in all its aspects is central. The process of unification is also a political liberation movement against restrictions which have to be abolished or overcome. And when the political unity of the nation is established, it represents and guarantees freedom.

Despite these obvious similarities between the two concepts of *Bildung* and nationalism there are of course differences of emphasis. So far, in talking about the political meaning of unity and freedom in nationalism, I have referred to the model of Western, especially French and American, nationalism. The differences in content between this model and the concept of *Bildung*, and furthermore the differences between Western nationalism and the German model of nationalism became manifest when German nationalism gained political momentum, incorporating at the same time the concept of *Bildung*. For this reason, these differences are better dealt with through concrete historical examples.

(3) In proceeding now to the historical development of the connection between *Bildung* and nationalism, I must make my systematic sketch relative. In the historical field we seldom find clear-cut distinctions between, for instance, universalism in accordance with the concept of *Bildung* and universalism in the sense of enlightened rationalism, or between political and cultural nationalism. Although one or other of the concepts usually is dominant in the work of a particular author, other strands of ideas are often intertwined. And frequently philosophers and writers changed or modified their concepts during their lifetime under the influence of their intellectual environment and of historical events. Hence one can say that there is no single, homogenous doctrine of nationalism in Germany, not least because of its involvement with the complex concept of *Bildung*. The dominant traits, which can be differentiated nonetheless, as well as some of the concrete historical formations, I want to sketch now with a few examples.

The concept of *Bildung* was first brought into contact with national self-consciousness (I do not yet want to use the term 'nationalism' in this context) by speculations about the nature of language.[25] On the foundations laid by Luther and the German Humanism of the sixteenth century, by

25 From here onward, cf. especially Kaiser, *Pietismus und Patriotismus im literarischen Deutschland*.

Jakob Böhme and Pietism as well as the German literature of the seventeenth and eighteenth centuries, Herder built up a theory of language which intensified the contacts and established a firm connection. To begin with, Herder attached language closely to the concept of *Bildung* as a process of individual self-realization. He defined language as "the organ of the powers of the soul, as the means of our innermost *Bildung* and education."[26] This combination of *Bildung* and language contains an important implication and suggests an equally important consequence. The definition implies that language is not regarded as a mere instrument. Indeed, in Herder's eyes, language is an active spiritual power that forms and even constitutes reality. The conception of the word as the divine creative *logos* is preserved in this understanding, although made immanent. If the concept of language as a general characteristic of human nature is left aside and attention is directed to the fact that there are different languages, the conclusion must be that each language, as an individual spiritual entity, embodies a different spirit or soul which both expresses and constitutes the spirit or soul of the people that speaks it. Hence the consequence of Herder's definition is twofold. From the viewpoint of language he concludes that "by means of its language a nation is educated and becomes *gebildet*,"[27] and from the viewpoint of the individual he considers that "we cannot be educated well except in the language of our people and our country."[28]

Herder thus located individual *Bildung* within the framework of the nation, now understood as a community constituted by the particular spirit of the common language. The universal element of *Bildung* was not lost, but universal unity had to be reached by way of *Bildung* within the individual nations. Only the combination of the manifold national individualities could establish the unity of humanity.

If the quality of language as a general characteristic of human nature is obliterated in favor of the differences between particular languages, the way is open to the conclusion that one language is richer, more differentiated, or more original than the other. On the assumption that languages embody

---

26 Johann Gottfried Herder, *Sämtliche Werke*, B. Suphan, ed., Berlin 1877–1913, vol. XVIII, pp. 157–158.
27 Ibid., vol. XVII, p. 287.
28 Ibid., vol. XVIII, pp. 157–158.

national spirits, this in turn might lead to the conclusion that the different qualities of languages represent different qualities of the national spirits und thus disclose the higher or lower value of the respective nations. Herder, it is true, did not draw this conclusion; he held the view that "no people is alone chosen by God," and that all peoples together, each in its place and with its own right, should work for the best of humanity.[29] But this view, reflecting enlightened humanism and a mystical vision of the unity of mankind, is not much more than a moral postulate.[30] We have to note that Herder's theory does allow, quite logically, the different conclusion indicated above.

This conclusion was drawn by Fichte. In his *Reden an die deutsche Nation*, he distinguished between original, unalloyed, and therefore vivid and vigorous languages like German, and languages like the Romance languages that he regarded as mixed together and therefore abstract and lifeless.[31] Accordingly the Latin peoples are regarded as mixed, the German as original, as an "*Urvolk*, the people as such."[32] The importance of being an original people and having an original language consists in the fact (this is where *Bildung* comes in again) that "life" and "spiritual *Bildung*" are not separated from each other but form a unity and thus establish the spiritual as well as the social unity of the people.[33]

With this argument Fichte not only claimed the superiority of the German people but also justified a German "mission" which was to lead to a "total transformation of the human race."[34] Nevertheless Fichte's pretension is not identical with the nationalistic or even racist justification of the German "mission" encountered later in the nineteenth century; although he was always invoked then. First, his argumentation is not yet *völkisch* in a biological sense, but rather spiritual and cultural, being based on his concept of language.[35] Secondly, the superiority of the German people does not lead by logical

29 Ibid., vol. XVII, p. 212.
30 Cf. Kaiser, *Pietismus und Patriotismus im literarischen Deutschland*, p. 216.
31 J. G. Fichte, *Reden an die deutsche Nation. Ausgewählte Werke*, vol. V, p. 430.
32 Ibid., p. 470.
33 Ibid., p. 438; cf. Pp. 387 seq. and 448.
34 Ibid., p. 511; cf. P. 547.
35 Cf. Klaus von See, *Die Ideen von 1789 und die Ideen von 1914. Völkisches Denken in Deutschland zwischen Französischer Revolution und Erstem Weltkrieg*, Frankfurt a. M. 1975, p. 17.

necessity to a national mission among other peoples. The universal human and political standards of Western nationalism can be fulfilled if everybody decides, through the strength of his free will, to realize them. On the other hand the paradigmatic quality of the German *Urvolk*, which is a natural entity, cannot be realized by an act of volition. Fichte does not explain how the German paradigm would transform mankind, but the claim to have a mission is made nonetheless, and with this claim his concept gains political momentum.

In my opinion Napoleon was the catalyst for the transformation of traditional patriotism and of the so-called concepts of cultural nationalism into political nationalism. The humiliating occupation of the German states by Napoleon made one goal appear paramount: the liberation of the German states from foreign rule. Fichte derived the certitude that this would be possible from his belief in the superiority of the German people over the French. The way to liberation could be achieved through *Bildung* as the means which unifies and hence strengthens the people. Although *Bildung* and life were not basically separated in his German *Urvolk*, he detected that foreign influence had led to partial disintegration and weakness.[36] Therefore *Bildung* in its true meaning, i.e., rooted in the people, had to be renewed. Through the employment of *Bildung* for a political aim, its universal aspects were overshadowed, and patriotism, which previously was bound to the territorial state and did not clash with enlightened humanism, was changed into a new kind of political nationalism.

A similar, although more complex process of change is shown in Ernst Moritz Arndt. Born and raised in Swedish Pomerania, he was a Swedish subject and originally confessed to patriotic feelings for the Swedish monarchy.[37] At the same time he presented himself as an enlightened cosmopolitan. In 1805 he wrote: "It is beautiful to love one's fatherland, but it is more beautiful to be a human being and hold everything human in higher esteem than the fatherland."[38] It required the defeat of Austria and Prussia in 1805 and 1806, as Arndt writes in his memoirs,[39] to awaken in him the wish for

---

36 J. G. Fichte, *Reden an die deutsche Nation. Ausgewählte Werke*, vol. V, pp. 387 seq. and 488.

37 E. M. Arndt, *Erinnerungen aus dem äußeren Leben*, p. 82.

38 Arndt, *Fragmente über Menschenbildung*, vol. II, Altona 1805, p. 202.

39 Arndt, *Erinnerungen*, p. 82.

the political unity of Germany. The basis for this unity and at the same time for the value of the German nation in comparison with others, he also found in German *Geist* and *Bildung*: "What Delphi was for the Greeks, Germania is for the new Europeans: the navel of the world of contemporary science and *Bildung*, the center of the innermost spiritual movements and forces."[40] But going beyond the cultural basis of national self-consciousness, he now demanded: "You must give a body to the spirit."[41]

Arndt's remarks on Germany as the spiritual center of Europe seem to reveal the well-known doctrine of German superiority. Indeed, in his booklet on the territorial army *(Landwehr)* he advises the officers to tell the young soldiers "that they are a much better and nobler people than the French."[42] But Arndt's position is more complicated than Fichte's. His advice has to be understood as instrumental; the feeling of superiority must be aroused in order to create enthusiasm for fighting. He advocated hate against the French, but at the same time confined hate against other peoples to the "lower instincts." On the higher level of virtue, science and art, he writes even in the year 1813, "hate against other peoples *(Volkshass)* ceases; here begins the great community of peoples, the general humanity, and here humanism and love, which make us children of One God and One Earth, will never be missing."[43] We have the paradoxical situation that on the one hand Arndt builds up political nationalism on the basis of national *Bildung*, while on the other hand he tries to preserve the universal elements of the concept of *Bildung*.

Arndt did not maintain this paradox. In 1848 he contributed to the discussion of the Polish question by stating that the Poles were inferior to the Germans.[44] His argumentation discloses that in the meantime he had assimilated Hegel's description of history as a process of *Bildung* of the

40 Arndt, *Hoffnungsrede vom Jahre 1810*, Erich Gülzow, ed., Greifswald 1921, p. 62.
41 Ibid., p. 55.
42 Arndt, *Was bedeutet Landsturm und Landwehr? Ausgewählte Werke*, Heinrich Meisner and Robert Geerds, eds., Leipzig n. d. (1913), vol. XIII, p. 90.
43 Arndt, *Über Volkshass und über den Gebrauch einer fremden Sprache*, Leipzig 1813, pp. 11, 12, 17, 20.
44 Arndt, "Polenlärm und Polenbegeisterung," *Werke*, vol. III: *Kleine Schriften*, A. Leffson and W. Steffens, eds., Berlin n. d., XII, pp. 178–180.

world spirit. Since the Poles have never created anything lasting in the realm of *Bildung*, he argued, they cannot claim any place in world history. Finally in 1854 he also adopted Fichte's concept of mixed and unalloyed peoples and even resorted to biological arguments by adducing the rapid increase of the German population as proof for the superiority of the German nation.[45] Arndt's ideological development reflects a general process which gradually added *völkische* and racist ideas to the cultural basis of German nationalism.

Let me go back once more to the Wars of Liberation. The numerous poems and pamphlets written on this occasion by Arndt, Körner, Schenkendorf, Brentano, Christian Stolberg and others, helped considerably to foster national self-consciousness in Germany. It is striking, however, that the nationalism which these writers articulated exhausted its political momentum in the struggle against Napoleon. When they spoke about "freedom," they always meant liberty from French domination. It is true that their notion of the "fatherland" went now beyond the territorial state they lived in and that they advocated the political unification of Germany; but political unification was primarily regarded as a means to liberation and as a guarantee of future independence. When it came to the question of the political constitution and inner structuring of the new national unity, there were either no clear and practical propositions, or they were silent. Most of them thought of Germany's unification in terms of a restoration of the empire, be it once more under the Habsburg dynasty, as Schenkendorf hoped, or under Prussian leadership, as Arndt would have preferred. The old problem of the tension between imperial representation and the territorial powers found no consideration. As far as the inner political constitution was concerned, there were at best ideas of a *ständische* order: Schenkendorf even wanted to revive the medieval order of society; Arndt advocated a more moderate and modern model, but still within this general framework.[46]

The reason why German nationalism did not adopt the political ideas of French nationalism lies in the fact that these ideas had been first

45 Arndt, *Pro Populo Germanico, Ernst Moritz Arndts Sämtliche Werke*, Magdeburg n. d., pp. 22, 141.
46 Cf. Günter Adam, *Die vaterländische Lyrik zur Zeit der Befreiungskriege* (Ph.D. Dissertation, Marburg 1962), pp. 85, 95, 97 seq., 101, 107, 110 seq.

discredited by the course of the French Revolution and then brought to Germany in the baggage of an army of occupation. On the other hand, the Germans could have resorted to the American model or developed ideas of the sovereignty of the people and representative government on their own. In my opinion an equally important reason for the rejection of such ideas has to be seen in the influence of the concept of *Bildung* on German nationalism, especially because of this concept's strong tension between a rather egocentric individualism and a very particular universalism. To put it pointedly: Between the preoccupation with deifying oneself and dreaming of a universal humanity of God-like individuals, not much room remained for pragmatic politics.

When Arndt in 1805 valued humanity higher than the fatherland, he considered the apolitical character of the Germans to be an advantage.[47] This view is familiar. To quote Schiller, for once, instead of Goethe: "Separated from political values," he wrote in 1801, "the German has established a particular value for himself. It is ethical greatness, it lives in the culture and in the character of the nation, which is independent from the nation's political fate."[48] And in his poem *Der Antritt des neuen Jahrhunderts* we find the line: "Freedom is only the realm of dreams."[49]

Thus, *Bildung* eclipsed pragmatic politics, and through its individual self-realization took the place of political emancipation. Its most far-reaching expression is to be found in Humboldt. In his eyes its highest form was an "inner *Bildung*,"[50] which worked for the "inner improvement and refinement"[51] of man and for the perfection of his "inner existence,"[52] his "inner essence."[53] Although after the defeat of Napoleon in 1814 he stated that the nation won the war through its own vigor and that the spirit of the nation therefore gained a greater vitality, his only conclusion

---

47 Cf. Rudolf Fahrner, *Arndt: Geistiges und politisches Verhalten*, Stuttgart 1937, p. 231.
48 Friedrich Schiller, "Deutsche Größe," *Sämtliche Werke*, Gerhard Fricke and Herbert G. Göpfert, eds., vol. I, 5th edition, München 1973, pp. 473–474.
49 Ibid., p. 459.
50 W. von Humboldt, *Werke*, vol. I, p. 238.
51 Ibid., p. 235.
52 Ibid., p. 60.
53 Ibid., p. 237.

was that the yearning "to take refuge in the solitude of science and art" could now be fulfilled.[54] Consequently, when he speaks about "freedom" as the "first and indispensable condition of *Bildung*," he means "inner freedom."[55] Participation in political life is regarded not only as secondary, but even as an obstacle to individual self-realization: "The human being must not be sacrificed for the citizen."[56] The state is expected to guarantee the realm of freedom, which *Bildung* requires, and "not to be concerned about the particular character of the individual existence," just as the individual for his part does not need to concern himself with the doings of the state.[57]

Humboldt's concept of *Bildung* aggravated the difficulties of bestowing a pragmatic political content on German nationalism. Nevertheless, in the course of the nineteenth century *Bildung* did assume political meaning with respect to the inner structuring of the nation, although only to a certain degree and in the particular way which the logic of the concept suggested.

In the years before and after the Wars of Liberation we have several so-called "organic" theories of the state in Germany. Adam Müller, for instance, projected a *ständische* order of the state in which aristocracy and middle-class would balance each other to mutual benefit, like contrasted pairs in living organisms.[58] Important in the present context is his characterization of the aristocracy as the female, conserving principle, and the middle class as the male, active principle. We find the very same identification in Ludwig Börne's *Kleine Gedanken über ständische Verfassung* (1818), except that he characterizes the active quality of the middle-class as the force of *Bildung*: "The life of the state is the product of a twofold force, of the

---

54 Ibid., p. 555.
55 Ibid., pp. 64, 235.
56 Ibid., p. 106.
57 Ibid., p.107.
58 Adam Müller, *Die Elemente der Staatskunst in Vorlesungen*, Berlin 1810; idem: *Von der Nothwendigkeit einer theologischen Grundlage der gesamten Staatswissenschaften und der Staatswirthschaft insbesondere*, Leipzig, 1820; cf. K. von See, *Die Ideen von 1789 und die Ideen von 1914*, p. 24; Ralph Reiner Wuthenow, "Romantik als Restauration bei Adam Heinrich Müller," *Katholizismus, konservative Kapitalismuskritik und Frühsozialismus bis 1850*, Albrecht Langner, ed., Paderborn and Wien 1975, pp. 75–97.

conserving instinct and the *Bildungstrieb*."[59] Müller and Börne regarded the two qualities or instincts as equally important, and accordingly also the two classes which represent them. But just as the different qualities of languages could lead to valuing a particular quality higher than others and consequently to regarding a particular language community as superior, so one could of course also value activity and dynamism higher than conservatism and thus believe in the superiority of the middle-class over other classes.

We can find the tendency to regard the middle-class as the most vital part of society already in Fichte and Arndt, although still interwoven with ideas of the true and simple people which included the peasants. During the middle decades of the nineteenth century the leading role of the middle-class was increasingly stressed, for instance by Wienberg and Gervinus.[60] In all these cases we can detect corresponding anti-feudal sentiments, more or less articulate. Outspoken opposition against the aristocracy was expressed by Gustav Freytag, and it was he who ascribed the leading role in society to the middle-class most decisively.

Freytag was a typical representative of the educated protestant, Prussian, and national-liberal middle-class after 1848, not least in terms of the inconsistencies to be found in his political and literary works. In his novel *Soll und Haben*, which is set in the Prussian border province of Silesia and in Poland, he showed himself a militant nationalist. On the other hand, like Arndt, he believed that no people can develop without spiritual exchange with other peoples, and from this higher standpoint he confessed to the idea of the "spiritual unity" of the "whole human race."[61]

With respect to the governing force of the social body he clearly decided in favor of dynamism and therefore regarded the middle-class as the true representative of the nation. In *Soll und Haben* the aristocracy is presented as a worn-out class which can no longer even play its conserving role and maintain its traditional position and property. Nevertheless,

59 Ludwig Börne, *Sämliche Schriften*, I. and P. Rippmann, eds., Dreieich 1977, vol. I, pp. 985–986, 988; cf. K. von See, *Die Ideen von 1789 und die Ideen von 1914*, p. 45.

60 K. von See, *Die Ideen von 1789 und die Ideen von 1914*, pp. 49, 50, 57.

61 Gustav Freytag, *Bilder aus der deutschen Vergangenheit*. Einleitung, *Gesammelte Werke*, 2nd series, vol. III, Leipzig n. d., p. 26; cf. pp. 24–25.

Freytag's anti-feudal feelings are not antagonistic; he stands rather for integration. At the end of his cycle of historical novels, *Die Ahnen*, the bourgeois hero and his sister marry the sister and brother of an aristocratic family— a telling renewal of the "mésalliances" which Goethe had already proposed as an ideal model of the future relation of the two classes at the end of *Wilhelm Meisters Lehrjahre*. Freytag's cycle of novels is revealing in more than one respect. It starts out in German prehistory and ends in 1848. Unlike the historical novels of the Romantic period it is not written to glorify the past, but to show where the history of the German nation is to lead and how it is to be fulfilled: The hero of the last part is a *Bildungsbürger*, a middle class intellectual who decides to become a journalist with the aim of leading society by way of influencing, or rather creating public opinion.

Thus, *Bildung* is of manifold significance in Freytag's opinion: It is still the vehicle of individual self-realization and, on a higher level, the constitutive basis of the nation which likewise is viewed as an individual body. Secondly it is seen as a dynamic force which is decisive for the development of the nation. Since the middle-class represents this force, this class is regarded as the true representative of the nation. But *Bildung* is also, thirdly, a means of integration, of establishing social unity; correspondingly the middle class is to absorb the other classes. Finally *Bildung* is an instrument to dominate society. Freytag was neither a supporter of the *ständische* order of society nor a real friend of parliamentary democracy.[62] What kind of concrete political system he would have preferred, is not very clear, except for one thing: He considered public opinion to be not only the means by which the nation finds its political articulation, but also the instrument "to firmly rein in the numerous demands of individuals and whole classes."[63] Considering the role Freytag ascribed to the journalist of his novel, as well as the fact that he was an influential political journalist himself, we cannot overlook the implicit political ambitions linked up with his concept of *Bildung*.

The inconsistencies between nationalism and intellectual humanism, between anti-feudalism and an ideology of social unity, between apolitical

---

62 Cf. Paul Ostwald, *Gustav Freytag als Politiker*, Berlin 1927; Walter Bussmann, "Gustav Freytag. Maßstäbe seiner Zeitkritik," *Archiv für Kulturgeschichte*, vol. 34 (1952), pp. 261–287.

63 Quoted from K. von See, *Die Ideen von 1789 und die Ideen von 1914*, p. 78.

inwardness and political ambitions by way of *Bildung*, continued to characterize a major part of the German intellectual class. Let me return, with some last remarks, to my starting point: The nationalistic exuberance of the intellectuals in World War I preserved these inconsistencies, although universal humanism disappeared and the accents shifted a little. The Hegelian philosopher Lasson saw the German spirit mainly characterized by its inwardness; at the same time he claimed the German engine of war to be an emanation of this spirit.[64] The historian Otto von Gierke gave reasons for the superiority of Germany by listing the achievements of her different classes and professions;[65] the fact that his honor roll is led by civil servants, professors, artists, and engineers (in this order), discloses a continuing hidden ambition for intellectual domination. The pastor Karl König believed that the war would unify religion and technology and thus recreate also a social unity rooted in the spirit.[66] If the Wars of Liberation had brought about the connection between nationalism and the concept of *Bildung*, World War I revealed the absurdity of its consequences.

64 Adolf Lasson, "Deutsche Art und deutsche Bildung," *Deutsche Reden in schwerer Zeit*, pp. 122–123, 138–139.
65 Otto von Gierke, "Krieg und Kultur," in *Deutsche Reden in schwerer Zeit*, p. 85.
66 Karl König, *Neue Kriegspredigten*, Jena, 1914, pp. 25, 38.

Apocalypticism, Hermeticism

Millenarianism, Hermeticism, and the Search for a Universal Science[1]

Previous essays in this collection have shown that the Scientific Revolution, the revival of Hermeticism, and a new sense of apocalyptic expectation were fundamental aspects of the intellectual ferment of the early modern period. The purpose of this essay is to demonstrate how apocalypticism and Hermeticism contribute to another key development in the seventeenth and eighteenth centuries—the search for a "universal science," that is, a holistic understanding of all spiritual, social, and natural phenomena which would enable modern man to comprehend, if not dominate, reality. The search for a universal science can be seen as a response to the differentiation and disintegration of sciences, but not of sciences alone. If reality in its different dimensions—nature, society, the human body and soul—is no longer experienced as a comprehensive whole, but as incoherent and independent realms of reality which require different instruments to deal with adequately, and if on top of that, the condition of one or the other of these disconnected realms seems unsatisfactory, there is even more reason to seek a universal instrument of knowledge which would encompass all dimensions of reality and heal any particular deficiencies.

It is not surprising that the seventeenth and eighteenth centuries were a period when such a longing for a universal science sprang up. The sciences, especially philosophy and the natural sciences, emancipated themselves from

1 Presented at a conference on "Science, Pseudo-Science, and Social Science" at the University of Florida, Gainesville, 1988 (first part); and at the Annual Meeting of the American History of Science Society, University of Florida, Gainesville, 1989 (second part).

First printed in *Science, Pseudo-Science, and Utopianism in Early Modern Thought.* Stephen A. McKnight, ed., Columbia and London: University of Missouri Press, 1992.

theology, which once had provided the ultimate answers to all questions. The natural sciences—in particular astronomy, physics, and mechanics—offered new insights into the structures and laws of material nature and set new standards for scientific objectivity and exactitude. A new philosophy developed which disconnected body and soul, body and reason, and dealt with the former in accordance with the mechanistic model. Other disciplines, like chemistry, medicine, and law, specialized more and more and gained independent prestige. Theology, by contrast, was clinging to orthodox dogmatism, which offered little to intelligent and open-minded Christians.

At the same time, the seventeenth and eighteenth centuries were a time of severe political and social grievances, which made the world seem to be deteriorating. Numerous wars, beginning with the Thirty Years' War, devastated Central Europe, particularly Germany. The Holy Roman Empire was, after the Thirty Years' War, not much more than a hollow shell; Germany disintegrated step by step into independent states. Within these states the rise of absolutism added to the grievances of the population. The subjects of the system of absolutism most often had reason to regard it as unjust and immoral. The peasants frequently were exploited or sold as soldiers; and the middle-class, which in the eighteenth century slowly recuperated from its losses in the Thirty Years' War and regained some self-esteem, was hindered from emancipating itself politically and socially. The churches, especially the Protestant church, were subjugated by the absolute state and made to serve its purposes. This induced many believers to defect and join sects or semi-independent denominations, especially pietist ones.

Thus, the concepts of a universal science which were developed during that period could have varied motives and, in consequence, different accents and scopes. Sometimes they were only by-products, as it were, of a more general, overriding longing for salvation. In the following I will outline, by way of example, two major versions of the concept of universal science, the first being motivated by the seemingly deficient state of the world, the second by the split between religious belief and scientific reason.

Universal Science as an Anticipation of the Millennium

From the twelfth to the eighteenth century there was a continuous tradition of millenarian movements in most of the West European countries, especially in Germany. Their endeavors usually combined the longing for spiritual salvation with political or social protest. During the time of the Reformation, this tradition, represented by movements like the Anabaptists or by apocalyptic prophets like Thomas Münzer, reached a critical point. The Protestant orthodoxy, which in the following centuries allied itself with the absolute state, warded off apocalyptic speculation, as the Catholic church always did. Nevertheless, this type of speculation flourished underneath the official doctrine, in Germany most often connected with Pietism. It was motivated by such grievances as mentioned above: spiritual dissatisfaction at the official church, political and social depression, crises and wars. In short, the authors of these apocalyptic visions and millenarian speculations regarded the present state of the world as being absolutely deficient, and they despaired of the meaning of history in general. As a consequence, they predicted that the world would come to an end soon and that the Sabbath of world history, the Millennium, would begin. They constructed a "course" in history, a "divine economy" underlying the seemingly inconsistent historical events and developments, in order to figure out the exact date of the beginning of the Millennium and in order to give meaning back to history. The seventeenth and eighteenth centuries are full of such prophecies and speculations. Their authors were learned men, most often pastors or professors of theology. Important representatives in Germany were Kuhlmann, Serrarius, Alsted, Comenius, Coccejus, Bengel, and Oetinger.

Since the millenarians devised their speculations on the course of history as comprehensive interpretations of the meaning of human existence in time, they tended to regard their systems as a key to all knowledge or to develop, with their visions of the Millennium, the concept of a universal science. The first millenarian to claim explicitly that his speculation on history would dominate all sciences was Quirinus Kuhlmann (1651-1689). Among the numerous visionaries who in the seventeenth century prophesied the imminent end of the world, he excelled particularly in missionary zeal. He tried to convince the princes of Germany as well as the theologians of the German universities that Germany had been chosen to prepare the world for the Final Judgment and for the universal renewal to take place in the "Fifth Monarchy." When he did not find acclaim in Germany, he traveled to almost all of the major residences in Europe – to London, Amsterdam, Paris, Constantinople, and Moscow – in order to offer salvation. In

Moscow, finally, he became a victim of his missionary fervor and was burnt as an agitator.

Kuhlmann found the basis of his speculation on history in the works of Jakob Böhme. He compiled Böhme's prophecies and related them to his own time in such a way that they seemed to be a confirmation of his speculation and its universal pretension: "From our Germany's new disciple of heaven I perceived my own arguments, which the Highest of All has marvelously shown to me, or rather solid proof of them, so that I intended, in honor of God and for the knowledge of men, after having exposed false doctrines, to enrich all sciences with many thousand inventions, and to disclose the difference between true and false Christian as well as heathen knowledge in a kind of doctrine hitherto unheard of, in which the great center of the world is hidden."[2]

After Kuhlmann the tendency grew even stronger to make the millenarian interpretation of history govern all sciences and to draw a future universal science from the comprehensive view of the world and history. The pastor and theologian Johann Albrecht Bengel (1687-1752) was convinced that he had gained knowledge of "things" and "times" through insights into the "divine economy."[3] This knowledge not only had theoretical value, but also conveyed an orientation of the present life toward the end of history: "By that the congregation of the Lord has a complete instruction so that always one can know where one stands."[4] Bengel had found out, by a complicated system of interpreting the Revelation of John, that the Millennium would begin in the year 1836. He was so overwhelmed by this knowledge of "times" that he did not draw any further conclusions for the knowledge of "things."

But Bengel's disciple Friedrich Christoph Oetinger (1702-1782) made the pretension explicit which Bengel's knowledge of "things" and "times" had contained only implicitly. Oetinger did not take pains to prove that the Millennium "was not far away anymore, because I take this as granted

2   Quirinus Kuhlmann, *Neubegeisterter Böhme: begreiffend hundertfünfzig Weissagungen*, Leiden 1647, p. 91. All translations of quotations from German sources are my own.
3   Johann Albrecht Bengel, *Erkläre Offenbarung Johannis*, p. 96.
4   Johann Albrecht Bengel, *Sechzig erbauliche Reden*, op. cit., p. 6.

by Bengel's calculation." He laid more stress on the necessity "that one gets prepared for it." And this preparation was to follow the "model of the Golden Age" (*die güldene Zeit*), as he called the Millennium.[5]

Oetinger designed the Millennium as a perfectly ordered society on this earth, with social equality, political justice, and moral integrity. This design reveals the motives behind the speculation: social, political, and moral protest against the conditions in the absolute state of his time. Oetinger formulated the description of the Millennium like a political program of general significance: "In any kingdom, true happiness has three conditions: first, that despite all multiplicity, which is not against order, and despite all differences of rank, the subjects have equality among each other, as we have learned from the distribution of Israel where the equal share of land reminded everybody not to pride himself above others. Everybody is to find his happiness in the happiness of his neighbor, his joy in the joy of all the other people, and by that everybody is to be a free lord among others; secondly, that they have a community of goods and not take delight in goods because they are a property; thirdly, that they demand nothing from each other as an obligation. Because, if everything would be available in abundance, there would be no need of government, property, and liabilities forced and extorted by government." Between the lines, Oetinger threatened the princes of Germany with the approaching end of history, and explicitly he admonished them, "on the grounds of getting prepared for the final period of time, to regard their subjects' welfare for their own, and to undertake reasonable reforms."[6]

So far, Oetinger's outlook on the Millennium reflected the political, social, and moral grievances of the time. But the matter did not rest there. His demand that we prepare ourselves "according to the model of the Golden Age" had an even wider meaning. In Oetinger's opinion the spiritual and social order of the Millennium would flow from a single principle, the "priesthood of Jesus," which Oetinger defined as "the basis and source of all true science." Thus, there would be only one science, which would

---

5   Friedrich Christoph Oetinger, "Die güldene Zeit" (1759), in *Abhandlungen von den letzten Dingen*, Karl Chr. Eberhard Ehmann, ed. Stuttgart, 1864, p. 7.

6   Ibid., pp. 29, 32.

comprise all sciences. And this universal science will be accessible for everybody by intuition, because Jesus will "present everything scientific very clearly and make it easily comprehensible, and he will abolish everything that is superfluous and confused in the sciences . . . all gifts of the spirit will be manifest." Therefore, the best preparation for the Millennium would be to lay the groundwork now for the future's universal science by abolishing the present fragmentation of the sciences. Oetinger deplored, in particular, the fragmentation of the sciences dealing with the physical nature of the world, with the order of society, and with the human body and soul: "With regard to the juridical science and the science which attends to the life of the body and soul, we propose to equalize what is uneven and humpy so that these three sciences, namely jurisprudence, theology, and medicine, are but one science out of one basic wisdom. Because the laceration of the sciences is a result of the corrupted time, the unification of the sciences is part of the preparation for the Golden Age."[7]

Later on, Oetinger added other sciences to his program of unification; he enumerates "the science of logic, which is the doctrine of reasoning, of ontology, which is the doctrine of general notions, of cosmology, which is the science of the world, of pneumatology, which is the science of the spirits, of psychology, the science of the soul, of theology, astronomy, physics, ethics, arithmetic, geometry, and algebra," and he predicts that "they all will stand together in perfection and intuitively will be seen by the children of God."[8]

The concept of the universal science anticipated spiritually the expected state of perfection. The universal science was to fulfill this function by comprising all dimensions of reality and by interpreting their meaning. Therefore, it would bring the state of deficiency to an end, at least in the consciousness of the adepts, and it would abolish ignorance, insecurity, and despair. It is important that this concept of a universal science was a result of a speculation on the meaning of history. Bengel and Oetinger understood history as a process of revelation which unfolds itself gradually until it reaches comprehensive knowledge of "things" and "times," and thus makes it possible, as Oetinger concluded, to devise a universal science.

7   Ibid., pp. 28, 141, 9.
8   Ibid., p. 139.

Bengel and Oetinger were of decisive influence on Schelling and Hegel.[9] Both Schelling and Hegel intended, although in different ways, a universal science as spiritual anticipation of perfection. In both cases this intention was a result of an interpretation of history, that is, the universal science was regarded as the manifestation of the meaning of history. Schelling repeated statements of Bengel and Oetinger almost literally when in 1804 he defined history as a "successively developing revelation of God,"[10] and like them he described the end of this process as the unification of all sciences, especially of the natural sciences with the humanities. In his view the universal science anticipates the state of perfection: "The peace of the Golden Age [*das Goldne Zeitalter*] will be made known first through the harmonious unification of all sciences."[11] Like apocalyptic visionaries, Schelling expected that this state would be reached soon; only "a short period of time" would pass until the universal science could be established: "It seems that it was reserved for our age to open the path to this objectivity of science."[12]

Hegel, also differing from Schelling in many respects, established the meaning of all being by means of a similar interpretation of history. For him history was a process of gradually developing revelation—that is, the process of self-realization of the spirit: "World history is . . . the exegesis and realization of the general spirit."[13] The individual consciousness, in this case Hegel's, partakes in this process and fulfills it insofar as it achieves the "absolute knowledge" of the philosophical system. In this state the subjective consciousness and the objective process of realization of the spirit are reconciled and the spirit grasps "the principle of unity of divine and human nature, the reconciliation of objective truth and freedom as appearing within self-consciousness and

9   See Ernst Benz, *Schellings theologische Geistesahnen*. Abhandlungen der Akademie der Wissenschaften und der Literatur in Mainz, no. 3, 1955; Ernst Benz, "Johann Albrecht Bengel und die Philosophie des deutschen Idealismus," in *Deutsche Vierteljahresschrift für Literaturwissenschaft und Geistesgeschichte* 27 (1953), pp. 509–528.

10 Friedrich Wilhelm Joseph Schelling, "Philosophie und Religion" (1804), in *Schellings Werke*. Manfred Schröter, ed. München 1927, vol. 4, p. 47.

11 Friedrich Wilhelm Joseph Schelling, "Die Weltalter" (1813), in *Schellings Werke*, vol. 4, p. 582.

12 Ibid., p. 581.

13 Georg Wilhelm Friedrich Hegel, *Grundlinien der Philosophie des Rechts*, Georg Lasson, ed., Leipzig 1911, § 342.

subjectivity."[14] Thus, the "absolute knowledge" of Hegel's philosophical system is meant to make the state of perfection and, consequently, the meaning of history spiritually manifest, and therefore can be regarded as a universal science.

Having the meaning of history expressed by a universal science was not confined to German thought. The idea of progress which aims at perfection and regards the spirit, be it divine or human, as the agent of progress, also developed in France in the eighteenth and nineteenth centuries. Condorcet, in his *Esquisse d'un tableau historique des progrès de l'esprit humain*, designed a universal science as the peak of progress of the human spirit and as the epitome of the final period of world history. In his view this science—that is, the new philosophy of *raison*—would become, on the basis of mathematical methods, a "universal instrument (*instrument universel*)," and this instrument would disclose the principles and universal truths which "determine the unchangeable and necessary laws of justice and injustice." Condorcet held the opinion that the "universal instrument" could "be applied to all matters of the human spirit."[15] A few decades later Auguste Comte determined the meaning of history to again be a process aiming at a universal science. After the sciences as well as the political constitutions of nations have passed through a "theological-fictitious" and a "metaphysical-abstract" period, they will arrive at the third and final state of "positivity," which is to be the universal instrument of the sciences as well as of the foundation of social order.[16] Also Marx and Engels, who resumed both German and French traditions, entertained the idea that the "pre-history of the human society" was close to its end. They further contended that a universal instrument would be developed at the end of this "pre-history"—namely, their dialectical and historical materialism—which would make the whole of human existence and of history intelligible.[17]

14   Georg Wilhelm Friedrich Hegel, *Phänomenologie des Geistes*, J. Hoffmeister, ed., Hamburg, 1952, pp. 26–28; Hegel, *Grundlinien der Philosophie des Rechts*, § 358.

15   Condorcet, *Esquisse d'un tableau historique des progrès de l'esprit humain: Entwurf einer historischen Darstellung der Fortschritte des menschlichen Geistes*, Wilhelm Alff, ed., Frankfurt 1963, pp. 267, 299.

16   Auguste Comte, *Cours de philosophie positive*, (1830–1842), E. Littré, ed., Paris 1864. For Condorcet's influence on Comte, see vol. 4, p. 185.

17   Karl Marx and Friedrich Engels, *Werke*, Berlin 1956, vol. 13, pp. 9–14.

The concepts of a universal science which originated in connection with or as a result of apocalyptic visions of the end of history and the beginning of the Millennium (or of the "Golden Age," the "Age of Positivism," the "Realm of Freedom") were rather pretentious. The authors of these visions were incorporated in their concepts: They were not only the illuminated prophets who foretold the end of the world; at the same time, and in consequence of their preview of the Millennium, they were the inaugurators of the new universal science "hitherto unheard of," as Kuhlmann put it. This high self-esteem and this pretension were the logical results of apocalyptic interpretations of the world and history. If the end is near and if one knows how the state of perfection will look, such a position suggests itself. However, this is not the only way of arriving at the concept of a universal science. There is another, more modest one, modest in the sense that its authors do not pretend to have insights "hitherto unheard of." On the contrary they want to renew an ancient knowledge. On the other hand, this variety of universal science holds pretensions, too, insofar it is supposed to be superior to and more comprehensive than the modern natural sciences.

Universal Science as a Renewal of Ancient Wisdom

Friedrich Wilhelm Joseph Schelling had prophesied a future objective science, reconciling the humanities and the natural sciences as a consequence of his speculation on history. In this respect he came close to the apocalyptic belief most clearly pronounced by Oetinger. On the other hand, Schelling also developed a more systematic theory about the unification of what was called at this time ontology, transcendental philosophy, and philosophy of nature. This systematic theory, which he did not bring to completion, was holistic, as we would say today. To a high degree it drew upon a tradition which sprang from different sources than the millenarian one: the tradition of Hermetic religion and philosophy. Also, Hermeticism was brought to Schelling's attention by Oetinger, who was an expert in all sorts of esoteric knowledge, although this connection has not yet been investigated satisfactorily.

Schelling's main intention was to overcome the split between the "Ego," or subject of cognition, and nature, or object of cognition. This split had dominated transcendental philosophy since Descartes and was maintained most sharply by Fichte in Schelling's time. Fichte defined nature as the "Non-Ego," which means that nature, as a mere object of our cognition, is not recognized as a reality of its own. Schelling realized that this theory makes nature appear as dead material with no other purpose than being used and dominated by us. He criticized Fichte for having made "egoism [*Ichheit*] the principle of philosophy," and for having reduced nature to a "mere mechanism." This theoretical understanding of nature, which in Schelling's eyes had governed "physics as a science" since Descartes, had the practical consequence that nature was subjugated to the destructive purposes of men, "because insofar as nature has to serve human purposes, it will be killed."[18]

In opposition to the dichotomic theory of cognition and the mechanistic theory of nature, Schelling developed an understanding of nature as a living and active cosmos which permanently produces and renews itself in the three potencies of matter, light, and organism by synthesizing its own polar forces of attraction and repulsion.[19] Human beings as the subject of cognition are participants in the comprehensive whole. This theory made use of major ideas of Hermeticism.

Schelling was not the only one in the decades around 1800 who took up the Hermetic tradition. Toward the end of the eighteenth century, there was growing dissatisfaction with the deepening split between traditional philosophy and the natural sciences, between theory of cognition and philosophy of nature, and also between science and religion. In this situation, Hermeticism was discovered, or rediscovered, as a worldview which again could integrate the conflicting perspectives. Goethe as a young man, for instance, was strongly influenced by the Hermetic tradition, which he used to forge both his own "personal religion" and a comprehensive, organic worldview.[20] The very first, however, to make extensive scholarly use of Hermeticism to bridge the gaps and ruptures which bothered so many intellectuals of the time, was Herder.

18 Friedrich Wilhelm Joseph v. Schelling, *Sämmtliche Werke*, ed. K. F. A. Schelling, Stuttgart 1856–1861, vol. 7, pp. 11, 17–19, 26–27, 108–112.
19 Ibid., vol. 4, pp. 13, 29–32. See *Klassiker der Naturphilosophie*, Gernot Böhme, ed., München 1989, pp. 247–255.
20 Rolf Christian Zimmermann, *Das Weltbild des jungen Goethe: Studien zur hermetischen Tradition des deutschen 18. Jahrhunderts*, 2 vols., München 1969 and 1979.

Johann Gottfried Herder was one of the most original and versatile minds in eighteenth-century Germany. He influenced his contemporaries (for instance, Goethe) and stimulated new developments in the literature and philosophy well into the next century. Despite his importance and the attention he has received, little note has been taken of the Hermetic influence on Herder or how his adaptation of Hermeticism influenced Romantic literature, the philosophy of nature (probably also Schelling's), and the philosophy of history.

It will be useful to give an impression of what Hermeticism meant in the seventeenth and eighteenth centuries, and how Herder encountered this tradition. The term Hermeticism refers to a religious and philosophical tradition which goes back to a collection of Greek scriptures from the end of the third century (in parts probably older): the *Corpus Hermeticum*. The central figure in these scriptures is "Thrice-Great Hermes" (Hermes Trismegistus), from whom the name of the collection as well as the doctrine was derived. Hermes is identified with the Egyptian god That, Thot, or Theut, the god of wisdom and inventor of numbers and writing. The Hermetic scriptures are presented as revelations of the god Hermes, or of the god Nous to Hermes, in order to give them the appearance of primordial wisdom. In fact, however, they are a syncretistic product of the first centuries A. D. which in many respects resembles Gnosticism. Before I describe the main characteristics of Hermeticism, I first want to show how it was transmitted into the eighteenth century and, in particular, to Herder.

Although Hermeticism was an esoteric doctrine, which for a long time lived in the intellectual underground, it never was entirely forgotten, not even in the Middle Ages. One reason for that was the attention paid to it by the church fathers Lactantius and Augustine. Lactantius regarded Hermes Trismegistus as one of the most important heathen prophets who lived prior to Pythagoras and Plato and prophesied Christianity.[21] Although Augustine condemned the Hermetic doctrine, he also held the opinion that Hermes was a seer of heathen antiquity "long before wise men and prophets came to the fore in Greece" and that he lived not much later than Moses.[22] These

---

21 Lucius Caecilius Firmianus Lactantius, *Divinarum institutionum libri VII. De ira Dei liber I*. Basileae 1532, *Div. Inst.* 1, 6; *De ira Dei* 11.
22 Aurelius Augustinus, *De Civitate Dei Libri XXII*, Bernardus Dombart and Alfonsus Kalb,eds., Stuttgart 1981, vol. 2, p. 315.

assessments had weight when Hermeticism was rediscovered in the Renaissance, because for the intellectuals of that time old age meant nearness to the sources of wisdom. When Cosimo de' Medici brought the Hermetic scriptures to Florence in 1460, he directed Marsilio Ficino to immediately translate the *Corpus* into Latin and to postpone the translation of the works of Plato which he had collected. The Hermetic doctrine was considered to be a *prisca theologia* (such was the term Ficino used in the introduction to his translation), a primordial and venerable theology, and Ficino called Hermes Trismegistus the "first author of theology," from which Orpheus, Pythagoras, and finally also Plato had derived their wisdom.[23] Ficino's translation of the *Corpus Hermeticum* was published in 1471 under the title *Pimander* (actually the title of the first book only), and from then on it enjoyed a continuous reception. By the end of the sixteenth century, it had gone through sixteen editions. Johann Albert Fabricius's *Bibliotheca Graeca* lists more than thirty editions from Ficino's translation of 1471 until the first translation into German of 1706. Most were in Latin, but there were also editions of the original Greek text and translations into other languages.

Ficino's characterization of the Hermetic doctrine as a *prisca theologia* was of great consequence; up to the eighteenth century it was accepted by many scholars, especially by those who were attracted by Hermeticism. Although the philologist Casaubon had proven as early as 1614 that the *Corpus Hermeticum* could not have been written before the beginning of Christianity, his findings did not dispel the conviction that in its essence the *Corpus* contained old Egyptian wisdom. Scholars of great, even international, reputation maintained this conviction.

The humanist Francesco Patrizi, editor of a collection of Hermetic writings, also published a major philosophical work influenced by Hermeticism, *Nova de universis philosophia* in 1591, before Casaubon's critique. He dedicated it to Pope Gregory XIV and even tried to have the traditional Aristotelian philosophy, legitimized by the Catholic Church, replaced by it. When in 1678 Ralph Cudworth, the intellectual doyen of the Cambridge Platonists, published his monumental work *The True Intellectual System of the Universe*, he could no longer ignore Casaubon's critique. His

---

23 Marsilio Ficino, *Opera Omnia, Basilea* 1576, 1836. See also Frances A. Yates, *Giordano Bruno and the Hermetic Tradition*, Chicago 1964, pp. 12–17.

work set standards for the scholarly assessment of the Hermetic scriptures throughout the following century. In their essence, Cudworth contended, the Hermetic texts were genuine "because, though they had been all forged by Christians never so much, yet being divulged in those ancient times, they must needs have something of the truth in them." And he concluded: "That there was anciently, amongst the Egyptians, such a man as *Thot*, *Theut*, or *Taut*, who, together with letters, was the first inventor of arts and sciences, as arithmetic, geometry . . . and of hieroglyphick learning, (therefore called by the Greeks *Hermes* and by the Latins *Mercurius*) cannot reasonably be denied."[24] Johann Albert Fabricius, whom his biographer called, even more than a century after his death, "one of the greatest polyhistors of the last century," dealt with the Hermetic scriptures in his multivolumed *Bibliotheca Graeca* of 1708 in the first volume, dedicated to authors *"qui ante homerum fuisse feruntur."*[25] The orientalist Jablonski, last but not least, depicted the old Egyptian religion in his *Pantheon Aegyptiorum* of 1752 by making use of the Hermetic scriptures.[26]

I have followed this line of transmission and influence in some detail because it also leads directly to Herder. Herder knew the works of the scholars mentioned above who were so familiar with Hermeticism and repeatedly quotes them in his book *Älteste Urkunde des Menschengeschlechts* of 1774, along with upright Hermeticists like Johann Georg Wachter and Johann Heinrich Ursin. In his library Herder had numerous Hermetic scriptures and works of authors who were inclined to Hermeticism—for example, an edition of the *Corpus Hermeticum* edited by Roselius in 1630, a *Fama mystica hermetica*, several works by Ursin, the complete works of Ficino and of both Picos della Mirandola, Campanella's *Philosophia universalis*, all theosophical works of Jakob Böhme, Colberg's *Platonisch-Hermetisches Christentum*, and the famous histories of heretics by Arnold and Mosheim. It is conspicuous how many heterodox or outright heretical works Herder's

24 Ralph Cudworth, *The True Intellectual System of the Universe*, London 1678, 1.4.18.
25 *Allgemeine Encyclopädie der Wissenschaften und Künste*, J. S. Ersch and J. G. Gruber, eds., vol. 40, part 2, Leipzig n. d. (after 1842), p. 69; *Ioannis Alberti Fabricii Bibliotheca Graeca*. Hamburg, 1708, vol. 1:1, pp. 46–80.
26 Paul Ernst Jablonski, *Pantheon Aegyptiorum*, op. cit., vol. 2:55, pp. 105–106.

library contained. At any rate, it is certain that Herder had a very good knowledge of Hermeticism. As early as 1765 there are allusions to Hermetic thoughts in Herder's writings and sermons.

Before I approach the question of how Herder was influenced by Hermetic thoughts, I have to briefly outline the main characteristics of Hermeticism. This can best be done by following the excellent account Ernest Lee Tuveson has given of the gist of the Hermetic doctrine.[27] In its classical form Hermeticism can be characterized as a religious worldview which holds a middle position between the Judeo-Christian and the pantheist conception of God and the world. With both of them Hermeticism has points of contact, as well as sharp contrasts. According to the Judeo-Christian belief, God is an extramundane being who created the world as an artifact. Although the human being as the *imago dei* shares certain attributes with God, the gap between God and the world is nonetheless absolute. It can only be bridged through revelations by the transcendent God, on whom human beings have no influence. In contrast, pantheism in its purest form, considers the whole cosmos to be divine and conceives of God as the totality of all being. The latter position is not very satisfying intellectually, for as Tuveson pointed out, "it actually amounts to saying nothing. If everything is God, it would be as meaningful to say nothing is God."[28] On the other hand, the Judeo-Christian conception is difficult to bear for many, because it means that the human beings are subjugated to the judgment of the transcendent God and can hope only for his mercy.

Hermeticism, in contrast, does not conceive of the world as an artifact created by God, but as a living organism in which God manifests himself as the body of the divine spirit, as it were, from which this spirit is distinct nonetheless. The human being cannot see the divine spirit, only his bodily manifestation in the world. This conception has been coined "panentheistic" by the German philosopher Krause in order to distinguish it from plain pantheism. It is a very attractive conception because it avoids making God identical with some animal or material object while it opens a path to salvation

---

27 Ernest Lee Tuveson, *The Avatars of Thrice Great Hermes: An Approach to Romanticism*, London 1982.

28 Ibid., p. 4.

which leads humans to God. Moreover, the *Corpus Hermeticum* holds that the world is contained within God's thoughts and is permeated by them. The thoughts of the humans are similar to God's for they can comprehend everything too. Hermes Trismegistus is instructed by the god Nous: "You are not hindered by anything to regard yourself as being immortal, as having knowledge of everything, of the arts, the sciences, morals, and of all animals. . . . Imagine that you are everywhere at the same time, on the earth, in the sea, in the sky; that you never were born, that you are still an embryo, that you are young, old, dead, and beyond death." The god Nous calls upon Hermes to comprehend everything, "the times, the places, the things, the qualities, the quantities—then you comprehend God." And to comprehend God means to become equal to God.[29] According to the Hermetic conviction, there is not only a likeness between human nature and God, in the Judeo-Christian sense of the *imago dei*, but also an analogous relationship between macrocosm and microcosm, between the divine spirit with his manifestations and the human mind with its thoughts, with its imagination. Although this conviction is not compatible with Christian belief—it also makes the saving function of Christ superfluous—many Christian philosophers and theologians tried again and again to reconcile Hermeticism with Christian belief, from Ficino, Pico della Mirandola, and Campanella, to Humanists like Patrizi, to the Christian Platonists Cudworth and More, Protestant theologians like Ursin, up to Herder.

The scriptures of the *Corpus Hermeticum* present their doctrine in a mythological imagery which is similar to the Gnostic one. But whereas Gnosis depicts a dualistic image of God and the world, the Hermetic one is analogous; it depicts the cosmos as a process of polar forces. The Hermeticist does not need to escape from the word in order to save himself; he wants to gain knowledge of the world in order to expand his own self, and utilize this knowledge to penetrate into the self of God. Hermeticism is a positive Gnosis, as it were, devoted to the world.

Hermeticism considers the cosmos (in modern terminology, "nature") to be a living organism and therefore views processes, which we understand as merely physical, in analogy to organic and even psychic

---

29 *Corpus Hermeticum*, book 11; quoted from *Hermès Trismégiste*, trans. Louis Menard, Paris 1983, pp. 78–79.

ones. Metal, for instance, can grow in the earth according to this view. There is sympathy between substances of the same kind, but antipathy between heterogeneous substances. This perception, along with the challenge to know God's manifestation in the cosmos, fostered the development of alchemical and magic practices. They revived in the Renaissance and were still exercised in the eighteenth century, particularly in medicine. Usually Hermetic magic and alchemy had nothing to do with occult sorcery but were attempts to discover the divine in nature through the laws of nature. Therefore, the Hermeticists could discard the mythological fundamentalism of the tradition without abandoning the essence of the Hermetic doctrine. Without major difficulties they could proceed from the medieval worldview to the Newtonian one. With their inclination to think in analogies between macrocosm and microcosm, and in the polar categories of attraction and repulsion, concentration and expansion, they even found themselves confirmed by the discoveries of the modern natural sciences. In the eighteenth century Hermeticism presented itself as religious worldview, which had the advantage that it did not need to resist the modern scientific image of the world, as the Christian churches did. This was the context in which Herder encountered Hermeticism.

The way Herder adopted the Hermetic tradition can best be seen in his book *Älteste Urkunde des Menschengeschlechts* (1774). At first view this work appears to be a new exegesis of the Book of Genesis, directed against fundamentalist as well as rationalistic interpretations of the Bible. Herder interprets the history of creation symbolically. He does not separate image and fact but assumes a symbolic meaning which comprises fact and meaning *within* the image of language. He understands the myth of creation as a historical document from the childhood of humankind, whose sensual mode of expression was in accordance with the way of thinking in oriental antiquity. And sensuality, in Herder's opinion, does not contradict truth; images do not exclude abstract theories.

This was an important new methodological development. Of equal importance, however, were the materials to which Herder applied his method. After a first chapter on the Book of Genesis, Herder describes what he calls the "holy sciences of the Egyptians" and what he derives from the *Corpus Hermeticum* and from the modern sources mentioned above. He concludes with a chapter on Greek philosophy, Gnosis, Cabala, and Zoroastrianism. On the face of it, Herder's considerations of religions and philosophies with similar symbolical expositions to those in the Book of Genesis appear to be an attempt to prove the great antiquity and truth of the latter. In fact, however, this line of argument relativizes the uniqueness of the biblical document. Nevertheless, I think this was not contrary to Herder's intentions. With his theory of symbolic meaning and the respective interpretations, Herder construes a primordial revelatory truth, a *prisca theologia*, which in the Hermetic religion found an expression of equal rank and antiquity to that in the Mosaic religion. Moreover, Herder's assessment was in line with a long tradition. Already Ficino, in his commentary to *Pimander*, had pointed out many parallels between the Book of Genesis and the Hermetic cosmogony. Above all, theses parallels were also emphasized by the Protestant and Hermeticist Johann Heinrich Ursin (1608-1667), to whom Herder referred frequently and of whose book *De Zoroastre bactriano, Hermete Trismegisto, etc.* he even had two copies in his library.

What did Herder's vision of the *prisca theologia*, which he deduced from the Book of Genesis as well as from the Hermetic tradition, look like? Herder interprets the six days of Creation and the Sabbath as a "great and significant *allegory* of God," with light, created on the first day, as the highest and most meaningful symbol.[30] The light is "the first beginning of creation, the oldest symbol and image of God, primordial image of all beauty, power, splendor, and goodness." The symbolic quality of the light is so significant because this symbol refers to spiritual as well as sensual and material phenomena, to nature as well as morality. Beyond that, the divine "Be light!" (as Herder translates, "*Sei Licht!*") is a symbol not only for the "stream of divinity and creativity through the whole of nature," but also for God's activity in history.[31] Herder constructs a network of analogies with correlations between polarities, and he sees the whole of creation with its relations between God, world, and human beings, between nature and history, comprehended by this network.

There is an even more concise symbol for the totality of creation which

---

30 Johann Gottfried Herder, *Sämmtliche Werke*, ed. Bernhard Suphan, Berlin 1877–1913, vol. 6, p. 278.
31 Ibid., pp. 222, 267, 449.

Herder finds in the Hermetic tradition in the "holy hieroglyph of Hermes." This "hieroglyph is indeed a very old symbol for the cosmos; it can be found among the most ancient petroglyphs. Herder could not abstain from charging it with some Hermetic magic of numbers and letters. However, what matters ultimately is the quintessential meaning of the "primordial symbol of Hermes," as Herder calls it: "One holy symbol: primordial image of creation, from which everything originated." This quintessential meaning is the Hermetic analogy between macrocosm and microcosm, the *aurea catena*, the golden chain of Hermeticism which embraces everything: "One in All! and All in One! one universe of formation (*Bildung*)! seed-corn out of which everything was to unfold, down the eternities!" The human being is, in Herder's words, "a magnificent chord of seven tones," "the image of the Whole in the shape and appearance (*Bildung*) of man: the great universe in the hieroglyph of the small!" He is "the image of God in all his powers, uses and attractions; at the same time he is the symbol and quintessence of the entire visible and invisible world."[32]

In *Älteste Urkunde des Menschengeschlechts* Herder disclosed the "genetic source" for his adaptation of Hermeticism. The religious and philosophical consequences of his adaptation he had already drawn before. In two essays written in 1769 (he was 25 years old then) he had laid down the general ideas of Hermetic panentheism. First, he presented the conception of the world as a manifestation of the divine spirit: "The power of God is omnipotent; he exerts his power over the universe which is his body: the body of his thoughts." Second, he made the analogy between human beings and God: God "is the idea, the power of the world: I am below him, like the earth is below the sun, but I have my own moon, too; my own sphere: I am a God in my world." His third principle was that everything is held together by the *aurea catena*: "I am real in the chain with God, just as I am in the chain with the worm on whim I tread with my feet."[33] In contrast to the worm, however, the human being can draw near to God and strive for perfection on the strength of his cognition, because the thoughts of human beings are, as parts of God's manifestation in the world, parts of God's thoughts and therefore an active power analogous to God's creative power.

32 Ibid., pp. 320–322, 340, 351, 365, 403.
33 Johann Gottfried Herder: "Grundsätze der Philosophie," *Euphorion* 54 (1960), p. 288.

Holy Hieroglyph of Hermes

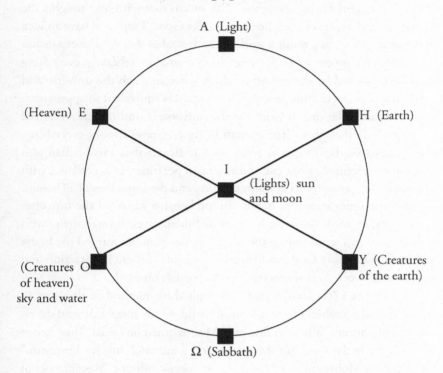

Correspondences:

7 days of creation
7 holy letters
7 planets
7 sciences
Shape of the human body
Features of the human face

In Herder's words, the human being "is a part of God's thoughts; a part of God's thoughts are his thoughts." This means that with his thoughts the human being has power over the universe like God: "I aspire to have an idea of the universe . . . as a result a world of bodies takes shape." The expansion of thoughts is a process of perfection: "In its formation (*Bildung*) everything must be explained by the thoughts which strive to reach the universe and are therefore perfect." This process of perfection is equivalent to approximation, even assimilation, to God, for the universe is nothing else than the body of God's thoughts: "The human being gravitates toward everything, even toward God." The term *gravitation* indicates that Herder had also adopted the Hermetic principle of thinking in polarities. In accordance with this principle, he interprets not only creation and the formation of all beings, but also the inner structure of the comprehensive whole of the universe: "Just as planets in the universe have formed themselves through the powers of attraction and repulsion: in the same way our soul has formed the body: and in the same way God has formed the world." "There is attraction and repulsion between us and everything which exists on earth."[34]

As early as 1769 Herder had also applied his method of thinking in analogies and polarities to the historical world, to the formation and development of nations. When he first read Montesquieu he noted: "Just as our soul fills the body: God fills the world: and a monarch fills his kingdom." He criticized Montesquieu's *L'esprit des lois* for not offering "metaphysics of the formation of nations." In Herder's opinion Montesquieu's notion of laws remained on the surface of institutions and could not grasp the inner laws of the living organism of nations. These inner laws, which penetrate the life of nations in all its dimensions, Herder found again in the principle of polarities, "in the laws of attraction and repulsion, which are natural to the character of a nation, which have originally formed this nation and maintained it in the same way as those laws have formed and maintained the body."[35] In his *Ideen zur Philosophie der Geschichte der Menschheit* (1784), Herder proceeded from the principle that the laws of history follow the "great analogy of nature" and that "the thoughts which God had revealed

---

34 Herder, *Sämmtliche Werke*, vol. 32, p. 229; "Grundsätze der Philosophie," pp. 229–231.
35 Ibid., vol. 4, pp. 467, 466, 469.

actively in his works every day" manifest themselves in history just as in nature. Therefore—and this is decisive—the laws can be discovered.[36]

In other writing of his middle period, Herder applies the principle of polarities, again on the strength of analogies, to human interrelationships. He uses this principle as a psychological instrument of cognition, as it were. Regarding attraction and repulsion of the bodies, Herder observes: "The great magnetism of nature, which attracts and repels" has "analogy with the human being." "In my opinion no psychology is possible which is not, with each step, a firm physiology." Again we can detect a typical characteristic of Hermeticism: Hermetic thinking tries to avoid dualism in the sense of radical antagonism between good and evil. Both powers are necessary; both sustain life: "Whoever cannot repel, cannot attract; both powers are but one pulsation of the soul." Another polarity, which Herder also uses very often in his psychological considerations, the polarity of concentration or contraction and expansion, makes this even more obvious. Herder translates this polarity as presumption and love, self-reliance and empathy. "Self-reliance and empathy (again: expansion and contraction) are the two expressions of the elasticity of our will." It does not escape Herder that presumption and self-reliance, if emphasized too much, can destroy humanity; therefore, this pole must form a field of tension with the opposite pole, but within this tension it is necessary: "Self-reliance is only to be the *conditio sine qua non*, the clod which keeps us in our place, not objects, but means. But a necessary means: because it is and it remains true that we love our neighbor only as we love ourselves. . . . The degree of the depth of our self-reliance is also the degree of our empathy with others." Once again Herder formulates the great credo of Hermeticism: "Look at the whole of nature, consider the great analogy of creation. . . . In short, follow nature!"[37]

In one of his last works, *Hermes und Poemander*, written one year before his death, Herder recapitulates his Hermetic worldview. This work imitates the dialogues between Hermes and Pimander in the *Corpus Hermeticum*; it is inserted into a treatise on the development of sciences in the seventeenth and eighteenth centuries, and it comments upon the new scientific discoveries in the symbolic language of the Hermetic myth. The astronomical

36 Ibid., vol. 13, p. 9.
37 Ibid., vol. 8, pp. 169–170, 47, 180; vol. 15, p. 325; vol. 8, pp. 199–201.

discoveries of Kepler and Newton and the mechanics and optics of the latter are, in Herder's eyes, corroborations of the Hermetic worldview, particularly of the principle of polarities. Attraction and repulsion, concentration and expansion, were, in Herder's words, "from ancient time the generating as well as sustaining central causes of the system of the universe; each age, each school applied its own terms and forms to the Whole. Newton's system defined the terms and forms most appropriate for his time with relations and numbers, without thereby explaining them."[38] In Herder's opinion, Newton used the instruments of modern sciences to describe the same truth which ancient Hermeticism had expressed already in the symbolic language of myth, and the mystery of this truth itself could not be explained in either form.

Herder takes the same view with respect to the scientific theories on the quality of light. Here, however, Herder does not follow Newton's hypothesis that space is a vacuum but holds to the older conception that space is filled with ether. It is not clear whether Herder was unaware or just kept silent about the fact that the *young* Newton had also subscribed to the ether hypothesis. Richard Westfall has shown that Newton, in his *Hypothesis Explaining the Properties of Light* (1675), presented this conception as a Hermetic cosmogony in the language of science.[39] Herder's view is almost identical with this conception. In his opinion space is not a vacuum, but filled with a "subtle, highly elastic ether" which can condense and vaporize.[40] Light does not emanate *from* the sun, but is produced through condensation of the ether *around* the sun. Newton even put forward the hypothesis that ether, in its different degrees of condensation, is the substance of all bodies, and that it produces, by means of perpetual condensation and vaporization, the cycle of becoming and vanishing. This sounded like the adoption of a central proposition of the *Corpus Hermeticum*, that the energies of the world are "composition and decomposition," and that nothing in the world gets lost.[41] In Newton's early theory ether assumed the role of a divine creative *quinta essencia*.

---

38 Ibid., vol. 23, p. 522.
39 Richard S. Westfall, "Newton and the Hermetic Tradition," in *Science, Medicine and Society in the Renaissance*, Allen G. Debus, ed., New York 1972, vol. 2, pp. 183–198.
40 Herder, *Sämmtliche Werke*, vol. 23, p. 536.
41 *Corpus Hermeticum*, book 11; quoted from *Hermès Trismégiste*, p. 71.

Herder ascribes the same role to light, through which "all life is sustained, perhaps also produced and propagated," although "the light as such . . . remains invisible for us." With this conception it is easy for Herder to draw again analogies to God, to creation, and to human beings: God's thoughts are invisible, like light as such, but they can be detected in the visible universe in which they are embodied; and this can be done by virtue of the instrument which is analogous to God's creativity, by virtue of "the most noble part of us that thinks, *our* light." With this sentence Herder refers back to his symbolical interpretation of light in *Älteste Urkunde des Menschengeschlechts*. In the dialogue *Hermes und Poemander* he comments through the mouth of Pimander upon the scientific discoveries of his time: "Pursue this golden chain of creation; it is an eternal becoming. Light is the silent agent of the ubiquitous deity which produces and always renews." "In the same way the light in yourself, your thoughts; it is always in a state of becoming." Finally, Herder puts in the mouth of Hermes the central conviction of modern Hermeticism: "I see that the most recent discoveries lead back to the most ancient philosophy, though the latter was shrouded in legends."[42]

The Hermetic worldview enabled Herder to be a modern, enlightened intellectual and to adopt the discoveries of modern sciences without being hindered by orthodox Christian belief. Nonetheless this worldview enabled him to consider himself as a faithful Christian because the Christian faith can be amalgamated with key ingredients of Hermeticism. The Hermetic worldview makes it possible to strive for godlike perfection by virtue of one's own power of cognition and still remain the child of the transcendent God. Hermeticism also makes it possible to explore the laws of nature and still look upon nature not as a dead matter, but as a living organism whose laws even apply to history. Finally, Hermeticism makes it possible to comprehend these laws symbolically and to understand ancient myths and the discoveries of modern sciences alike as equivalent expressions of the same truth, of a *philosophia perennis*.

Herder's Hermetic worldview contributed to a new conception of nature and human nature: of nature as a living, even animated, organism in which the divine is embodied, and of the human being not only as a

42 Herder, *Sämmtliche Werke*, vol. 23, pp. 528–535.

creature and part of nature, but also as godlike creator. So far it has not been sufficiently appreciated that this conception of Hermeticism influenced the new German anthropology and philosophy of nature of the late eighteenth century and gave new impulses to the search for a universal science.

Apocalyptic Activism:
Ernst Jünger on the Meaning of the First World War[1]

"War, the father of everything, is our father, too; he has hammered, chiseled and hardened us to what we are. And ever, as long as the spinning wheel of life turns within us, this war will be the axis around which it circles."[2] These sentences open the introduction to Jünger's essay *Fighting as an Inner Experience (Der Kampf als inneres Erlebnis)*, published in 1922. And indeed, the war experience between 1914 and 1918 is the central existential event that dominates the writings of Jünger between 1920 and 1932, from *Storm of Steel (In Stahlgewittern)* up to *The Worker (Der Arbeiter)*. Although the representation of the war experience becomes more general and abstract, extending to historical and philosophical reflections, the war remains the pivot. His view of the world, of politics, society and culture, is never able to break out of the perspective formed by the war experience.

A few years ago, the original diary that was the basis of Jünger's first book, *Storm of Steel*, was published. The editor, Helmuth Kiesel, wrote in his epilogue: "There is hardly another diary that documents the First World War for such a long time and with such consistency from the perspective

---

1 Originally published under the title, "Planetary Consequences: Ernst Jünger on the Meaning of the First World War." It was presented at the International Conference on "Ernst Jünger: Writing and War," Minerva Institute for German History, Tel Aviv University, 2014. First printed in Tel Aviver Jahrbuch für deutsche Geschichte, Vol. 44 (2016): *Deutsche Offiziere. Militarismus und die Akteure der Gewalt.* Galili Shahar, ed. Göttingen. Wallstein Verlag, 2016.

2 Ernst Jünger, *Der Kampf als inneres Erlebnis.* Berlin 1922, p. 2. All translations of quotations from Jünger's works—as well as translations of other German sources—are my own, except translations of quotations from *In Stahlgewittern*; here I quote from the English translation *Storm of Steel*, translated with an introduction by Michael Hofmann. New York, 2003.

of a front-line officer [...]. Personal notes stand next to military commentaries, amorous remarks next to martial ones, sentimental entries next to barbaric ones, touching utterances next to repulsive ones."[3] Although the published book condensed the diary considerably, some events were depicted in more detail, some of the more factual and prosaic notes were dramatized, reflections were added. The style was improved in general, the diary was turned into 'literature', as it were. However, the published book preserves, even intensifies, some of the disturbing and horrifying experiences the volunteer Jünger endured, experiences of the war as an alien, eerie reality that with terrifying suddenness breaks into normal everyday life and destroys it. This is how Jünger describes the first day after his arrival behind the front in *Storm of Steel*. The soldiers, who have been billeted at a village school, are peacefully eating breakfast when a shell suddenly explodes, wounding and killing several men.

"What was that about? War had shown its claws, and stripped off its mask of coziness. It was all so strange, so impersonal. We had barely begun to think about the enemy, that mysterious, treacherous being somewhere. This event so far beyond anything we had experienced, made such a powerful impression on us that it was difficult to understand what had happened. It was like a ghostly manifestation in broad daylight."[4]

This reflection was not part of the original diary, but was added in the published version. In retrospect, Jünger notes that this incident left a "decisive impression."[5] Indeed, characteristic aspects of the war experience are inserted into this event as Jünger reflects on it. In contrast to the order and security of the world as it was experienced until 1914, the war appears as absolute chaos, its devastating power as blind and "impersonal," especially because of its technical manifestation. The chaotic force disorients soldiers, making them isolated and helpless. Everything is "strange"—"it was difficult to understand what had happened"—the war in its totality is beyond comprehension, the meaning of killing and dying remains obscure.

3   Ernst Jünger, *Kriegstagebuch 1914–1918*. Helmuth Kiesel, ed. Stuttgart, 2010, p. 596.
4   Ernst Jünger, *In Stahlgewittern. Aus dem Tagebuch eines Stoßtruppführers*. 2nd ed. Berlin 1922 (first ed. 1920), p. 2; quoted from *Storm of Steel*., p. 7.
5   In *Stahlgewittern*, p. 2; *Storm of Steel*, p. 6,

The question of the meaning of the war occupied Jünger's mind throughout the 1920s. "What was our role in the war, and what did the war mean for us?" he asks in *Fighting as an Inner Experience*.[6] The answer, that all the suffering and dying might have been without meaning, is hard to bear. Jünger comes close to this thought when he speaks of the "mad futility" of the terrible devastations,[7] but in the end he cannot accept it. Therefore, meaning has to be found, a meaning that can drive away the alarming thought of meaninglessness and aimlessness. Between *Fighting as an Inner Experience* and *The Worker*, Jünger's answers changed.

The national camp had a ready answer which not only gave meaning to the soldiers' death—"They died so that Germany may live"—but was also able to interpret the meaning of Germany's defeat. Franz Schauwecker, a 'national revolutionary' and an acquaintance of Jünger's, summed up this interpretation in a succinct formula at the end of his novel *Rising of the Nation (Aufbruch der Nation)*: "We had to lose the war in order to win the nation."[8]

At first, Jünger shared the nationalistic viewpoint when he considered the meaning of war for a people in general. In *Fighting as an Inner Experience* he writes: "Each people has its own culture whose possibilities can flourish only on the sharply limited ground of this culture. If one nevertheless speaks, for instance, of a Western culture, one does it with the same right as one designates a host of animals as insects."[9] Hence Jünger concludes that each people has an "unlimited and reckless will to save and augment its interest," which means "the will to fight" against other peoples.[10]

But around the mid-twenties the nationalistic interpretation of the war became too narrow for Jünger. He developed a perspective that comprised both the single soldier, his fighting, killing and dying in the battle, and the World War in general as a historical event. This perspective distinguished him more and more from the national camp and from most of the "conservative revolutionaries"; in the end, with *The Worker*, it made him a

---

6   *Der Kampf als inneres Erlebnis*, p. 3.
7   Ibid., p. 16.
8   Franz Schauwecker, *Aufbruch der Nation*. Berlin 1930, p. 403.
9   *Der Kampf als inneres Erlebnis*, p. 37 seq.
10 Ibid.

maverick. An important reason for Jünger's change of view was most probably the war experience itself, the fact that on both sides of the front the
soldiers had equal experiences of suffering and dying. In his essay *Fire and
Blood (Feuer und Blut)* of 1925 Jünger writes: "Certainly we stand closer to
the enemy of race than to any pacifist and internationalist. And certainly
we accomplish, by killing each other here, something more important than
if we fused into a big mishmash. We create together *one* piece of work, and
our workshop is the battle."[11] These remarks presage Jünger's endeavors of
the following years to comprehend the war as an event with meaning for
civilization as such and with "planetary" consequences.[12]

Between 1920 and 1932 Jünger developed two major patterns of interpretation. The first one is a-historic and defines war as a law of nature.
Already in *Storm of Steel* Jünger describes the devastating power of modern
long-range weapons as the eruption of forces of nature. In *Fighting as an
Inner Experience* he compares war to the sexual impulse and calls it a "law
of nature";[13] in *Fire and Blood* he sees war as being ruled by the "eternal
laws of nature."[14] As late as 1930, in the beginning of his essay *The Total
Mobilization (Die totale Mobimachung)*, he compares the wars of different
epochs to volcanoes, "in which always the same innermost natural fire
erupts." He modifies his statement, however, by saying that these volcanoes
"are at work in very different territories," and declares his present intention
"to collect some data that distinguish the last war, our war, the greatest and
most effective event of this time, from other wars whose histories have been
transmitted to us."[15]

With this statement Jünger brings a second pattern of interpretation
into the foreground, a pattern that is basically incompatible with the first
as it belongs to the field of cultural theory or even philosophy of history—
one that interprets the war as a special *historical* event with particular *historical* consequences. This pattern of interpretation dominates the

11 Ernst Jünger, *Feuer und Blut. Ein kleiner Ausschnitt aus einer großen Schlacht.*
    Magdeburg, 1925, p. 52.
12 Ernst Jünger, *Der Arbeiter. Herrschaft und Gestalt.* Hamburg, 1932, pp. 151,
    210, 232.
13 *Der Kampf als inneres Erlebnis*, p. 36.
14 *Feuer und Blut*, p. 51.
15 Ernst Jünger, *Die totale Mobilmachung.* Berlin, 1931, p. 3.

subsequent, and in my view more significant, essay *The Worker* of 1932, which I will now consider in more detail. I will return later to the question whether it is indeed incompatible with the first pattern of interpretation.

Jünger's description of the particular nature of the World War as a historical event presents the war as an apocalyptic turning point. Jünger's second pattern of interpretation, which takes the form of historical speculation, has, at the same time, an apocalyptic structure. The notion of apocalypse is a particular way of interpreting the world and history; it has a specific structure, characteristic elements of interpretation as well as characteristic language symbols. While the apocalyptic interpretation of history is of Jewish and Christian origin, in modernity it has become detached from its original religious sources. This is also the case with regard to Jünger's speculation, but the structural, formal and linguistic correspondences between the original religious and the modern secular apocalyptic interpretations are striking. The central structural characteristic of the apocalypse is the link between fall and renewal, destruction and redemption. The notion of the apocalypse enables experiences of deficiency and loss of meaning, of suffering and destruction, to be understood as part of a process in which the *whole world*, the 'old world' of the past is doomed to death. According to this interpretation, the 'old world' has to be totally destroyed so that a 'new world', a fundamentally changed reality, can emerge. The apocalypse expresses a strict dualistic world view, also in the moral sense; and this world view unfolds as a speculation on history, on the time 'before' and 'after' the turning point in world history. The apocalyptic visionary sees himself on the brink of this turning point. But there is a great difference between the religious apocalypse of the Judeo-Christian tradition and the modern, secular apocalypse insofar as the former envisions that God will intervene in history, execute the last judgment and grant salvation in a *heavenly* Jerusalem, whereas the latter urges the people to execute the destruction of the old world themselves and to engineer the change to a radically new existence.

There were many apocalyptic interpretations of the First World War in Germany, both during and after the war, and in different ideological camps. The apocalypse is neither left nor right; it can be filled with different ideological or political content. In the national camp of the 1920s the most popular interpretation accorded with Schauwecker's, namely that all the sacrifices were necessary for the rebirth of the German nation. The National Socialists adopted this interpretation; after 1933 they could claim that now, with the Third Reich, the rebirth had come.

Jünger's apocalyptic world view is not nationalistic; he fills the pattern of interpretation with different content. At the beginning of his reflections on the war he does not yet know precisely what this content will be. But already in *Fighting as an Inner Experience* he sees the war as a "turning point in world history"; and the apocalyptic symbolism of destruction, change, and salvation forces itself upon him, in his own words, "decay, fermentation, resurrection.." And further: "Why is it that our time is teeming with forces, devastating as well as generating forces? Why does it bear such untold promise in its womb? Many things may die in fever; at the same time the same flame brews up prospects and wonders in a thousand retorts."[16]

Eight years later, in *The Total Mobilization*, the apocalyptic content of Jünger's interpretation is clearly manifest. The war is now seen definitely as a historical event, i.e., as a unique event of world-historic importance, "of equal rank to the French Revolution."[17] The result of the "catastrophe," Jünger determines, is of a "strict historical consequence."[18] In his eyes, progress, "the big People's Church of the nineteenth century,"[19] has gained a new quality because of the war; it takes the devastating power of the war even further and crushes the remains of the old world. For Jünger, the destruction that the war has made total now opens the prospect for the new mode of existence: "the magnified image of a gigantic process of work."[20]

The essay *The Worker* amplifies this thought and develops it into a grand speculation on history; the book is the sum of Jünger's efforts to interpret the meaning of the war. *The Worker* appears to be a sober diagnosis of the time; on first view it seems that the author seems to be portraying the political, social and cultural tendencies of his time dispassionately and lucidly. He observes that the world of the nineteenth century has collapsed, bourgeois society is "condemned to death." Individualism, with its values, its

---

16 *Der Kampf als inneres Erlebnis*, p. 1.
17 *Die totale Mobilmachung*, p. 6.
18 Ibid., p. 18.
19 Ibid., p. 9.
20 Ibid., p. 6.

morals, its concept of liberal freedom, has become obsolete. The reverse process, which abolishes individualism, is the "typification" of living conditions. The individual whose identity was rooted in the distinctiveness and uniqueness of his existence has been replaced by the new figure of the "type." The "type" seeks "characteristics that are rooted beyond individual existence."[21] The typification of living conditions corresponds to "the victorious march of technology." Technology has become the dominating creative power of the modern world, which permeates and changes all working and living conditions.[22] In accordance with these developments a new concept of work has emerged, which is fundamentally different from that of the nineteenth century. The new concept of work is total, it knows "no opposition outside itself." There is no occupation that cannot be understood as work; even sports and leisure time are nothing but prolongations of the world of work, not its opposite. The "worker," who is part of this new world, is defined neither professionally nor economically, nor socially; he is the heroic fighter of the World War, transferred from the battlefield to the sphere of production as his new workshop. The worker, because of his war experience, has a "new relationship with the elementary."[23] He is, after all, a new type of human being who uses technology as "a means of total revolution" and who thereby strives for a new order: "the realization of the world's character as total work."[24]

Yet this seemingly objective summary conceals an apocalyptic interpretation, which is manifest, first of all, by the structure of the universal "worldview" that Jünger infers from his observations. He interprets the supersession of the *bourgeois* world by other social conditions and forms of life as a "planetary" process that expresses a fundamental antagonism, namely "the difference between two epochs, one of which that is coming into existence devours the other one that is coming to an end."[25] He conceives of himself and his time as being at the turning point from the old to the new world. In his eyes, as well as in the opinion of his apocalyptic

---

21 *Der Arbeiter*, pp. 21, 138.
22 Ibid., p. 160.
23 Ibid., p. 203.
24 Ibid., pp. 86 sq., 162, 169.
25 Ibid., pp. 210, 232, 151.

contemporaries, the present crisis is pregnant with the new existence; and this crisis has been inaugurated by the First World War. The phenomena he observes center on the war experience as in a focal point: The First World War has started a process of destruction that continues after the war's end and is going to achieve global meaning: "The whole world is covered by the rubble of demolished images. We participate in the spectacle of a decline that can be compared only with geological catastrophes."[26] The First World War has accelerated the "victorious march of technology" in murderous fashion. It has deprived the soldiers of their individuality and shaped them into the "type." It has turned the warriors' duel into the technical "work" of impersonal destruction. Therefore, in his book Jünger returns again and again to the war in order to illustrate his "worldview."

The apocalyptic character of this worldview becomes even more evident if Jünger's valuations and intentions are uncovered. He pretends to strike a sober balance, and he stresses that "our task is *seeing*, not valuing,"[27] but in fact he deceives his readers. The legend of the dispassionate diagnostician and indifferent seismograph, propagated by Jünger himself and by uncritical interpreters, should not mislead us. Jünger in fact views the decline of the *bourgeois* epoch not unemotionally and objectively, but with satisfaction. He welcomes this decline, as all apocalyptic visionaries welcome the destruction of the old world. In the act of destruction Jünger finds "the fiery source of a new vitality,"[28] and he intends to consummate the work of destruction and to extend it to the intellectual foundations, valuations, and entire education of the bourgeois epoch. This intention is pleasurable: "To take part in this blasting operation is one of the sublime and cruel delights of our time."[29]

The motive of Jünger's will to destruction is also apocalyptic. He longs for the fall of the old world "as preparation for a new and more valiant life."[30] There is no doubt that the loss of meaning that Jünger observed among his contemporaries was also experienced by himself: "One could

26 Ibid., p. 74.
27 Ibid., p. 130.
28 Ibid., p. 152.
29 Ibid., p. 40.
30 Ibid.

assemble entire libraries in which in thousandfold variations resonates the lamentation of man who suddenly sees himself attacked from invisible zones and who sees himself stripped of his meaning and his potency in every respect. This is the great and only theme of the literature that deals with decline and doom."[31] And Jünger reacts with an apocalyptic vision, with the vision of a "new human race."[32]

Jünger attains his image of the new world and the new human being by consenting to the developments he observes, by accepting them as "historically dominant," and by pushing them to the extreme: since the world of the nineteenth century has collapsed in the First World War, the spirit and morals of the past are obsolete and must be destroyed completely; since the sphere of work tends to intrude into all other spheres of life, Jünger projects a future "total state of work,"[33] since the technological civilization results in a loss of individuality, Jünger consents to "the attack on individual existence" and accepts the "type" as the figure of the new human being.[34] In this way Jünger creates the impression thar if he merely determines the facts objectively and draws the inevitable conclusions, he can project an apocalyptic vision. With the demand "to increase the impact and speed of the processes in which we are involved," he can even express the impulse of apocalyptic activism and nonetheless claim that he is reasoning only in accordance with the historically dominant developments. In retrospect Jünger confirmed that he was interested not only in dispassionate knowledge. In 1963, in the foreword to the new edition of *The Worker* he wrote: "The book presented, and still presents, the attempt to gain a vantage point from which the manifold and even antagonistic events could not only be understood, but also—although dangerous—be welcomed."[35]

The will not only to understand the tendencies of the time, but to accept them and even put oneself at their head is, in Jünger's eyes, "heroic realism."[36] The "heroism" of this attitude lies in the willingness to submit to

31 Ibid., p. 144.
32 Ibid., p. 162.
33 Ibid., p. 235.
34 Ibid., p. 151.
35 Ernst Jünger, *Der Arbeiter. Werke*, 6. Stuttgart n.d. (1963), p. 11.
36 *Der Arbeiter* (1932), pp. 34, 170.

the seemingly historically dominant developments. Jünger sees this willingness realized in an exemplary way by the "unknown soldier" of the World War.[37] In *Fire and Blood*, Jünger already describes the new form of heroism as "recognizing as our own personal will what fate demands."[38] In *The Worker* this attitude is ascribed to the figure of the "type" as his cardinal virtue.

This interpretation reveals an existential dimension, in addition to the speculation on history. The vision of the apocalypse, motivated by experiences of meaninglessness and decline, claims to answer also the question of existential meaning. What gain does Jünger promise the new existence of the worker? And what is the price that has to be paid for apocalyptic salvation? The gain is power, freedom and pleasure; the price is acquiescence in the loss of individuality, the readiness to sacrifice oneself: "Thus it would be rewarding to watch how the individual man under heroic aspects appears, on the one hand, as the unknown soldier who is destroyed on the battlefields of work, and how he therefore, on the other hand, comes forward as the master and organizer of the world, as a commanding type in the possession of a plenitude of power that hitherto could only vaguely be surmised. Both sides belong to the figure of the worker, and this is what basically unites them even when they measure themselves against each other in deadly fighting."[39]

The new man whom Jünger designates as "the figure of the worker" is merely the perfect synthesis of doer and victim in self-sacrifice. The individual human being is absorbed in this figure; even as doer, he must realize the "sacrifice of the self." The reward for the self-sacrifice is—apart from "possession of a plenitude of power"—the feeling of absolute freedom that anticipates salvation. In order to reach the vantage point "from which freedom can be perceived," the doer must accept that the "destruction whose extent cannot yet be foreseen" takes hold of him, too. The "freedom of the doer" is "accomplished not before it is recognized as the expression of necessity,"[40] and the necessity inherent in the deed, when raised to something

37   Ibid., pp. 40 sq.
38   *Feuer und Blut*, p. 49.
39 · *Der Arbeiter* (1932), pp. 40 sq.
40   Ibid., p. 57.

absolute, is the readiness also to endure the deed, the readiness to sacrifice oneself. If the doer achieves this attitude, which is free of determination, he can even feel pleasure in his self-sacrifice, pleasure as a foretaste of salvation. Then he belongs to that race of men "who can blow themselves up with pleasure and who still can see in this act a confirmation of order."[41]

The characteristics of the worker portrayed by Jünger comprise a new concept of apocalyptic activism. It is a paradoxical form of apocalypse in which—with the synthesis of doer and victim—destruction and salvation are also made identical. And there is a second paradoxical phenomenon that leads back to the apparent incompatibility between an a-historic interpretation of the war and a speculation on history that follows the model of the apocalypse. The apocalyptic act, raised to something absolute, which comprises action as well as self-sacrifice, again reveals "the elementary" as an instinctive, if not cosmic, "primordial power" that is in fact a-historic.[42] The apocalyptic speculation, produced by the desire to interpret history, paradoxically dissolves history in the act of apocalyptic change. The hitherto existing history is destroyed together with the "old world"; it sinks into the darkness of indifference. The worker as the typical figure of the "new human race" can thus be understood as a representative of the "post-histoire," *avant la lettre.*

41   Ibid., p. 34.
42   Ibid., pp. 198, 203.

Transhumanism:
The Final Revolution[1]

From St. Paul and St. Augustine to the Renaissance and further on to the utopian speculations and ideological programs of modern times, the idea of a "new man" or "new human being" has played an important role as a symbol expressing the hope for a radical transformation of human existence. The revolutionary movements of the last two centuries, in particular, projected a "new human being'" that would harmonize with the ideological plans for a "new society" morally, socially, and politically. The means that were used to make people conform to the idea of the "new human being" were education, indoctrination, and coercion. It is well known that the ideological and political attempts to create a "new human being" were not successful and, at the worst, led to concentration camps, gulags, and even to mass murder.

During the last three decades new visions of a radical structural change of the human condition have developed, based on the truly revolutionary progress in computer science and computer technology, as well as in biochemistry and genetics. Although these visions have been generated by scientific progress, it is often difficult to tell whether they still belong to the realm of science or are just science fiction. Stephan Vladimir Bugaj, who identifies himself as a writer, filmmaker and philosopher, formerly vice-director of IntelliGenesis, a company that explored artificial intelligence,[2] observed

1   Presented at the International Conference on "Revolutions: Finished and Unfinished, From Primal to Final," University of Hong Kong, 2010. First printed in *Revolutions: Finished and Unfinished, From Primal to Final.* Paul Caringella, Wayne Cristaudo, Glenn Hughes, eds. Newcastle upon Tyne: Cambridge Scholars Publishing, 2012.

2   Http://www.linkedin.com/in/bugaj; accessed 29 January 2010.

some time ago that the border between science fiction and "serious" science has become permeable.[3] Writers thoroughly study the newest developments in the pertinent sciences; Margaret Atwood, for instance, demonstrated profound knowledge of genetics in her novel *Oryx and Crake*. On the other side, specialists in computer theory and technology gain inspiration from film and literature, for instance from the 'cyberpunk' literature of authors like William Gibson, who coined the term 'cyberspace' in his novel *Neuromancer*.[4] Ray Kurzweil, computer specialist and inventor, who is advertised as "a leading futurist and transhumanist,"[5] sees science fiction films as "always a good source for inventing the future."[6] Some authors of science fiction novels even have a professional background, like Gregory Benford, who is Professor of Astrophysics and Plasmaphysics at the University of California at Irvine. Other scientists write science books for a general public, like Hans Moravec, Professor and Principal Research Scientist at the Robotics Institute of Carnegie Mellon University in Pittsburgh. All cybernauts or cyberates—as Bugaj calls these people moving in the inter-space between science and science fiction—have no problems combining technology and fantasy.

Now, what are the characteristics of the "new human being" designed by scientists as well as by authors of science fiction? Max More, founder and president of the Extropy Institute and mastermind of the "evolving transhumanist philosophy of extropy," provides a fairly concise answer. In 1998 he published a *Transhumanist Declaration* with seven *Extropian Principles*. Some of these principles sound sensible and do not go beyond traditional humanist and democratic values, like "Open Society—Supporting social orders that foster freedom of speech," or "Self-Direction—Seeking independent thinking, individual freedom, personal responsibility, self-direction, self-esteem, and respect

3 Stephan Vladimir Bugaj, "Was liest die Zukunft?" in *Frankfurter Allgemeine Zeitung*, 17 April 2001, p. 54.

4 William Gibson, *Neuromancer*. New York ,1984, pp. 46, 51.

5 "Guest Post: David Orban Reviews Singulariry Summit 2009." Http://singu-larityhub.com/2009/10/05/guest-post-david-orban—reviews-singularity-sum-mit-2009/; Accessed 20 October 2009.

6 Ray Kurzweil, *The Age of Spiritual Machines: How We Will Live, Work and Think in the New Age of Intelligent Machines*. London, 1999, p. 143.

for others."[7] The general goal, however, clearly transcends the traditional idea of the human condition: "Transhumanists take humanism further by challenging human limits by means of science and technology combined with critical and creative thinking. We challenge the inevitability of aging and death, and we seek continuing enhancements of our intellectual abilities, our physical capacities, and our emotional development. We see humanity as a transitory stage in the evolutionary development of intelligence. We advocate using science to accelerate our move from human to a transhuman or posthuman condition."[8] This will be possible, More believes, by "integrating our intelligent technology into ourselves in a posthuman synthesis."[9] The process of integration, however, works the other way round, most cybernauts believe, namely as decoding the brain and downloading the mind onto a computer.

In his book *Mind Children*, Hans Moravec describes in detail how a robot brain surgeon opens the skull of a human being, simulates the brain layer after layer, then excavates it. Eventually the skull is empty, the body dies. The "mind has been removed from the brain and transferred to a machine."[10] Now, what do we gain from such a procedure? The goal, as we know from Max More and other transhumanists, is to enhance our intellectual abilities and to challenge the inevitability of aging and death. Compared with genetic engineering, transferring the mind to a computer has the advantage that it becomes independent from protein and faster than neurons, because neurons "which can now switch less than a thousand times per second" never can compete with "the billions-per-second speed of even today's computer components." This means that "a genetically engineered superhuman would be just a second-rate kind of robot, designed under the handicap that its construction can only be by DNA-guided protein synthesis. Only in the eyes of human chauvinists would it have an advantage—

7   Max More, "The Extropian Principles. Version 3.0. A Transhumanist Declaratio," (1998). http://www.maxmore.com/extprn3.htm; p. 2; Accessed 12 March 2001.
8   Ibid., p. 1.
9   Ibid., p. 6.
10 Hans Moravec, *Mind Children: The Future of Robot and Human Intelligence.* Cambridge, Mass. and London, 1988, p. 110.

because it retains more of the original human limitations than other robots."[11]

In comparison, the computerized new human being has no limitations. The mind that merges with the data universe of the computers achieves ubiquity; it can be everywhere at the same time, it expands into the universe; the limits of time and space are abolished. At the same time, it transcends individuality and becomes immortal, being no longer protein-based. In Moravec's words: "Concepts of life, death, and identity will lose their present meaning as your mental fragments and those of others are combined, shuffled, and recombined into temporary associations, sometimes large, sometimes small, sometimes long isolated and highly individual, at other times ephemeral, mere ripples on the rapids of civilization's torrent of knowledge."[12]

In recent years, much publicity has been accorded Ray Kurzweil's prediction on how artificial intelligence will develop in the future. Probably his prognosis was so successful because he presented it with literary means. In his book *The Age of Spiritual Machines: How We Will Live, Work and Think in the New Age of Intelligent Machines*, first published in 1999, the author engages in a dialogue with a fictitious artificial intelligence on several stages of its future development: in the years 2009, 2019, 2029, and 2099. The themes of these dialogues are not only technological questions, but also ordinary human needs and feelings: how one lives as an artificial intelligence, how bodily needs can be articulated and satisfied, especially sexual needs, what career one can pursue, how much money one can make and what one can afford from one's income, whether one can still consume material goods, etc.

Kurzweil's speculation goes in the same direction as Moravec's, but is even more wide-ranging. The first step, similar to Moravec's vision, consists of "scanning a human brain" and "copying its neural circuitry in a neural computer."[13] Kurzweil expects that "destructive scanning [as Moravec describes it] will be feasible early in the twenty-first century. Noninvasive scanning with sufficient resolution and bandwidth will take longer but will be

11 Ibid., p. 108.
12 Ibid., p. 115.
13 Kurzweil, *The Age of Spiritual Machines*, p. 3.

feasible by the end of the first half of the twenty-first century."[14] As early as 2029, "human cognition is being ported to machines, and many machines have personalities, skills, and knowledge bases derived from the reverse engineering of human intelligence." This means: "A sharp division no longer exists between the human world and the machine world."[15] In 2099 the border between physical and virtual reality will disappear, as well as the border between individual consciousness and the data universe. Like Moravec, Kurzweil expects that "the identity issue" is "no longer an issue," so that—as the artificial intelligence of 2099 explains—"it became clear that counting individual persons wasn't too meaningful."[16] The "software-based intelligence" is non-individual, but also can become personal; it "is able to manifest bodies at will: one or more virtual bodies at different levels of virtual reality and nanoengineered physical bodies using instantly reconfigurable nanobot swarms."[17] In general, however, this "transhuman being" "exists as software,"[18] which means that it is immaterial.

Becoming immaterial is valued as a kind of redemption. In a German science fiction novel the "project of spirit without body" is called a "Gnostic project."[19] Indeed, the speculations about dematerializing the human mind are pure Gnostic fantasies of redemption: liberation of the divine *pneuma* from the prison of the body and the material world. Jeff Zaleski, a contributing editor of *Publishers Weekly*, described precisely the Gnostic driving force in a conversation with John Perry Barlow, author of the *Declaration of the Independence of Cyberspace*: "There's an idea that is achieving common coinage on the Net: that the Net is somehow going to free us from the tyranny of the body, and of the material world in general—that we are souls trapped in physical reality and that by going digital we can break free of the prison of the flesh."[20]

14   Ibid., p. 316, note 4; cf. Ray Kurzweil, *The Singularity Is Near: When Humans Transcend Biology*. New York, 2005, pp. 157–167.

15   Kurzweil, *The Age of Spiritual Machines*, p. 222.

16   Ibid., pp. 242–243.

17   Ibid., p. 234.

18   Ibid., p. 247.

19   Jens Johler and Olaf-Axel Burow, *Gottes Gehirn*. Hamburg and Vienna, 2001, p. 268.

20   Jeff Zaleski, *The Soul of Cyberspace: How New Technology Is Changing Our Spiritual Lives*. San Francisco ,1997, p. 35.

The benefit that immaterial existence promises is immortality; Kurzweil predicts that by the year 2099 "life expectancy is no longer a variable term in relation to intelligent beings."[21] But immortality is not enough. Some masterminds of cyberspace like Barlow or Mark Pesce ascribe godlike character to the global consciousness that will be generated by the universal networking of computers.[22] Individual consciousness could participate in this divine quality by connecting itself with the global consciousness. "Transhuman," then, turns out to be a synonym for "godlike." In Bugaj's eyes, "the godlike search for a new form of intelligent life" is a greater philosophical challenge than most other aspects of the cyber-world, and he bluntly states: "Many cyberates are governed by the desire to get beyond mere humanness and become a god."[23]

What does it mean to become a god? It means to become omnipotent. If computer technology is combined with nanotechnology, this vision could become true, as Zaleski speculates: "Nanotechnology is coming and, in theory, promises a godlike dominion over matter, for through it we may be able to build anything whose atomic structure we can describe—including, in time, brains of any or every sort."[24] Or bodies, of course, too, one can add with Kurzweil, so that the software-based transhuman being can drink a glass of wine once in a while.

But let's not be satirical. The whole matter is highly ambivalent. There can be no doubt that recent developments in computer technology and robotics, nanotechnology and genetics have brought valuable progress to our technological civilization, have improved our everyday lives, have improved health care and even produced new possibilities to cure or to ease certain diseases. Speech recognition technology for the blind has been developed. Some varieties of blindness can be partly cured with the help of electrodes and computer technology. In a similar way, people who suffer from some kind of paralysis can retrieve command of their movements. People with locked-in syndrome or motor neuron disease like Stephen W. Hawking (amyotrophic lateral sclerosis—ALS) can communicate with the

21 Kurzweil, *The Age of Spiritual Machines*, p. 280.
22 Zaleski, *The Soul of Cyberspace*, pp. 27–49, 134–153, 180–195, 235–261.
23 Bugaj, "Was liest die Zukunft?" p. 54. Translation my own.
24 Zaleski, *The Soul of Cyberspace*, p. 152.

help of advanced computer technology. Robots perform surgery where the human hand would not be steady or precise enough. Discoveries in genetics are helping to fight some varieties of cancer. And so on.

The ambivalence characterizing the new technologies and the speculations about their future development is spectacularly represented by Ray Kurzweil. Kurzweil made meritorious contributions to computer technology. As early as in 1976, he invented the "Kurzweil Reading Machine" which reads text to blind people. In 2005 he introduced the much more advanced reading machine "Kurzweil-National Federation of the Blind Reader." He improved the capability and quality of electronic music synthesizers, inspired by his friend Stevie Wonder. In 1987 he came forward with the world's first large-vocabulary speech recognition program; and in 1996 he developed a new pattern-recognition-based computer technology to help people with various disabilities. These and other inventions and developments earned him many awards. In 1998, for instance, he received the "Inventor of the Year" award from the Massachusetts Institute of Technology. In the following year President Bill Clinton honored him with the "National Medal of Technology." In 2001 he received the Lemelson – MIT Prize for a lifetime of developing technologies to help the disabled and to enrich the arts. Kurzweil has received honorary doctor degrees from sixteen universities and colleges.[25]

On the other hand, there are these visions and prophecies that are hard to digest for anyone who is not an ardent member of the cyberspace community. Kurzweil believes that the innovation rate of computer technology is increasing not linearly but exponentially. In consequence, artificial intelligence will surpass human intelligence at some point; Kurzweil calls this point "singularity." In his latest book of 2005, *The Singularity Is Near*, a *New York Times* bestselling book, he prophesies the singularity for 2045.[26] In 2009, he became co-founder and chancellor of the Singularity University at Mountain View. In cooperation with nearby Google and the NASA Ames Research Center, this university will research and foster the development of exponentially advancing technologies. Kurzweil, born in 1948,

25 Http://en.wikipedia.org/wiki/Raymond_Kurzweil; Accesses on 31 Janurary 2010, pp. 2–6.
26 Kurzweil, *The Singularity Is Near*, pp. 5–9, 136.

hopes to live until the singularity happens in 2045, because he assumes that the exponentially advanced computer technology of that time, assisted by nanotechnology, will slow down the aging process, then reverse it, and finally make him immortal. In order to survive until 2045, Kurzweil swallows 250 supplement pills every day, drinks ten glasses of alkaline water, 10 cups of green tea, but also several glasses of red wine a week, and on weekends he undergoes intravenous transfusions of chemical cocktails in order to reprogram his biochemistry.[27] In case of an earlier death, Kurzweil's body will be chemically preserved, frozen in liquid nitrogen, and stored at a facility of the Alcor Life Extension Foundation, "in the hope that future medical technology will be able to revive him."[28]

All this is pretty bizarre. Pulitzer Prize winner Douglas Hofstadter characterized the ambivalence of Kurzweil's work and also of Moravec's books with a drastic comparison: "It's as if you took a lot of very good food and some dog excrement and blended it all up so that you can't possibly figure out what's good or bad. It's an intimate mixture of rubbish and good ideas, and it's very hard to disentangle the two, because these are smart people; they're not stupid."[29] Whether you agree with this critique depends on whether or not you think it is desirable to become immortal and lead a virtual existence without a body. Because this is the revolutionary driving force behind the concept of 'transhumanism', as Max More put it in his *Transhumanist Declaration*: "We do not accept the undesirable aspects of the human condition."[30] Albert Camus has characterized such an attitude as "metaphysical rebellion": "Metaphysical rebellion is the movement by which man protests against his condition and against the whole of creation. It is metaphysical because it contests the ends of man and of creation."[31]

27 Http://en.wikipedia.org/wiki/Raymond_Kurzweil; Accessed 31 January 2010, pp. 9–10; Thomas Thiel, "Wenn der Kühlschrank zweimal klingelt. Die Singularity University bereitet mit Googles Hilfe auf den Moment vor, an dem Maschinen die intellektuelle Vorherrschaft übernehmen," in *Frankfurter Allgemeine Zeitung*, 16 December 2009.

28 Ibid., p. 10.

29 Ibid., p. 11.

30 More, "The Extropian Principles," p. 3.

31 Albert Camus, *The Rebel: An Essay on Man in Revolt*. New York, 1956, p. 23.

National Socialism and Political Religion

Spiritual Revolution and Magic: Speculation and Political Action in National Socialism[1]

It might cause surprise to find the term "magic" being used in connection with National Socialism.[2] If I am not mistaken, this term embraces a wide scale of meanings in the English language which range from sorcery or witchcraft, from mysterious and seemingly inexplicable, even supernatural powers, to the mere skill of producing baffling effects or illusions. Hence it

1   Presented at the Vanderbilt Conference on Gnosticism and Modernity, Vanderbilt University, Nashville, 1978. First published in *Modern Age*. Vol. 23, No. 4, Fall 1979.

2   The persisting confusion surrounding the terms "National Socialism" and "Fascism" leads me to emphasize that my article deals with National Socialism, not with Fascism, and that when I mention Fascism I mean Italian Fascism. Recent studies, especially those of Renzo De Felice (*Le interpretazioni del fascismo*, 2nd edition, Bari 1970; *Intervista sul fascismo*, Roma – Bari, 1975; and his biography *Mussolini*, in four volumes, Torino, 1965 seq.), have shown that the differences between National Socialism and Fascism are greater than their similarities, such that it seems questionable to include both historical phenomena, let alone a host of others, under the term "Fascism." The question is of course of great interest if the ideological and political movements of Fascism and National Socialism can each be viewed as a coherent epochal phenomenon of the first half of our century. But this question gets obscured by inadequate terminology, especially if the term "Fascism" is used as a theoretical concept, such as in all kinds of "theories of Fascism." In what follows, I cannot go into this matter in greater detail. What I want to stress here is that I use the terms "National Socialism" and "Fascism" as language symbols that belong to the historical reality of the movements which produced them for the purposes of self-interpretation, and therefore as such they do not explain anything theoretically.

is not only possible to speak of the magic charms of a sorcerer, or the magic powers of demons, but also of the magic of love, and even of the magic tricks of an illusionist. Because of all these possible connotations, it happens only too easily that associations lead into wrong directions when the term "magic" is applied to National Socialism. It is the same case with the German language. When I first interpreted certain characteristics of National Socialism as "magical,"[3] I was frequently misunderstood as attempting to "demonize" National Socialism, to say nothing of the role I presumably had assigned to Hitler. The image of Hitler as a "demon" was indeed cherished by some German historians in the fifties and sixties, for it allowed them to refrain from a rational analysis of the man, the reason for his success, and the monstrous deeds of his regime. Of course my concept of magic has nothing to do with this kind of demonology or other seemingly inexplicable occult powers. It is, on the contrary, indispensable for an adequate theoretical analysis.

Before I try to give an account of what "magic" means in relation to National Socialism, I want to deal with another problem which is of importance in this context. In recent years, considerable attention has been paid to the question of whether or not National Socialism was a revolutionary movement and whether or not it inaugurated a revolution in 1933. In my opinion, this question is related to the interpretation of National Socialism as a "magical" phenomenon. I hope to provide a better approach to this interpretation, which is still irritating for many, by going into the problem of revolution first.

In the epilogue to my book *Magie und Manipulation* I ventured the thesis that National Socialism tried to alter social reality not by means of a revolution, but through magic. This certainly was a rather pointed statement which sounded strange to many ears. That National Socialism was not a revolutionary movement and that in 1933 no revolution took place was nevertheless a widely accepted opinion, and it still is today. If one judges the incidents of 1933 and 1934 by the paradigm of a typical modern revolution like the Russian one, as I did then myself, one has indeed to register a different degree of political and social transformation. As to the ideology

3   Klaus Vondung, *Magie und Manipulation. Ideologischer Kult und politische Religion des Nationalsozialismus*, Göttingen, 1971.

and the impetus of the movement, Camus established that National Socialists were very different from the "classical revolutionaries," because "instead of divinizing reason they chose to divinize irrationalism," and because, despite their endeavor to build up a world empire, "they lacked the ambition of universality which is rooted in the belief that reason will gain the victory."[4] (The autonomous and instrumental reason is meant in this case and not reason in the classical or Christian sense.) And quite recently the foremost expert on Fascism, Renzo De Felice, has contended that Fascism, to be sure, was a revolutionary movement which to a certain extent stood in the tradition of 1789, which had a concept of progress and was "determined to change society and the individual person to a degree never before attempted nor realized," but that in contrast National Socialism was not revolutionary at all but traditional, regressive, mystical.[5]

It is in fact De Felice's new interpretation of Fascism as well as some recent English and American studies on National Socialism (in particular those of J. P. Stern and George L. Mosse[6]) that have helped me to clarify and differentiate my own evaluation of National Socialism. I still take the view that elements of magical speculation and action were inherent in National Socialism, but I have now reached the conclusion that these elements also had a revolutionary character. It is true that Hitler's seizure of power in 1933 was not a revolution in the same sense as the one of October 1917, that National Socialism was not a revolutionary movement according to the standard set up by Camus, and that there may even be fundamental differences between National Socialism and Fascism, which would bring the latter closer to progressivist movements; but all of these characterizations do not exhaust the definition of the word "revolution."

National Socialism usually is not accepted as a revolutionary movement because the term "revolution" is reserved, as for instance by Camus and De Felice, for ideologies and political movements in the tradition of the

---

4   Albert Camus, *L'homme révolté*, Paris 1951; quoted from the German translation *Der Mensch in der Revolte*, Reinbek, 1969, p. 145. (Unless otherwise acknowledged, all translations of quotations are my own.)

5   Renzo De Felice, *Der Faschismus*, Stuttgart, 1977, p. 46, cf. Pp. 99–102.

6   J. P. Stern, *Hitler. The Führer and the People*, Berkeley – Los Angeles, 1975; George L. Mosse, *The Nationalization of the Masses*, New York, 1975.

Enlightenment and the French Revolution: progressivism, positivism, communism, anarchism. National Socialism, on the other hand, is placed in the tradition of nationalistic and racist ideologies whose sources are found in German Romanticism and the Nationalism of the Napoleonic era. Numerous scholars have investigated this tradition;[7] they all put emphasis on its irrationalism, racist nationalism, and anti-modernism in contrast to the rationalism, universalism and belief in progress of "true" revolutionary movements, and therefore classify it as reactionary and regressive. But such studies do not sufficiently penetrate the screen of symbols like *Volk*, *Volksgeist*, *Volksgemeinschaft*, *Rasse* and *Blut*; they do not see clearly what processes of consciousness took place behind the established symbols and, above all, what effects these phenomena of consciousness had on attitudes and actions. What happened in this development from Fichte via Arndt, Lagarde, and Langbehn to Hitler (to mention only a few representative names) was, in a word, the breakthrough of a "spiritual revolution" to magic action whose characteristics were revolutionary indeed.

Jürgen Gebhardt has shown that in the decades before and after 1800 thinkers like Hegel, the Schlegel brothers, Schelling, Fichte and others developed the concept of a "spiritual revolution" (*Revolution des Geistes*), following the tradition of Christian-gnostic speculations on self-redemption and in reaction to the French Revolution.[8] This spiritual substitute for a political revolution was meant to lead beyond political emancipation to complete human self-realization in the sense of a world-immanent "redemption." It culminated in the "revolutionary desire to actualize the Kingdom of God."[9] This program aimed inward, toward revolutionizing consciousness, and after the political revolution of 1848/49 had failed, this retreat into inwardness (*Innerlichkeit*) grew even stronger. But the revolutionary impulse

7   Cf. Hans Kohn, *The Mind of Germany: The Education of a Nation*, New York, 1960; Fritz Stern, *The Politics of Cultural Despair*, Berkeley – Los Angeles, 1961; Georg Lukács, *Die Zerstörung der Vernunft*, Neuwied – Berlin, 1962; George L. Mosse, *The Crisis of German Ideology: Intellectual Origins oft the Third Reich*, New York, 1964.

8   Jürgen Gebhardt, "Zur Physiognomie einer Epoche," in *Die Revolution des Geistes. Politisches Denken in Deutschland 1770–1830*, Jürgen Gebhardt, ed., München 1968, pp. 7–16.

9   Friedrich Schlegel, *Athenaeum*, reprint Stuttgart 1960, p. 236.

was nevertheless maintained. It became manifest when, toward the end of the nineteenth century and under the impact of a crisis which affected the German society as a whole but in particular the traditional intellectual class (*Bildungsbürgertum*), these programs of self-redemption were not only radicalized and, indeed, vulgarized as well, but also turned into programs of social action by all sorts of reformist and "third way" movements which have been rightly gathered under the term "revolt of the intellectuals" (*Gebildeten-Revolte*).[10]

It was also during this time that the most radical part of the *Gebildeten-Revolte* laid the ideological foundations of National Socialism. This is well known, but the terms "conservative," "reactionary" or "regressive" which are usually employed to characterize this movement fall short of catching its essence. The *Gebildeten-Revolte* had little in common with classic conservatism and its idea of a Christian and patriarchal order of society. It is true that this movement's protest against modern civilization showed regressive traits; the protest was indeed a reaction against industrialization and its negative consequences for the traditional *Bildungsbürgertum*. But in the Third Reich, anti-modernism, though still a major ideological feature, did not have a very great effect, and certainly did not bring Germany's social order back to pre-modern times. A much stronger motive for the radicalization of the spiritual revolution was the experience of social disintegration and, in its context, the decline of the political influence and social status of the *Bildungsbürgertum*. Hence models of a new social order were developed. The symbol *Volksgemeinschaft*, understood as a "new community," expressed the striving toward a fundamental structural change of society; the symbols "race" and "new man" gave voice to the aspiration for a transformation of human nature. Both of these aspirations might well be called "revolutionary," to say the least.

De Felice accounts for the revolutionary character of Fascism by referring to its attempt to create a new type of human being, and he contends that National Socialism did not develop such an idea.[11] This thesis is, in

10   Cf. Ulrich Linse, "Die Jugendkulturbewegung," *Das Wilhelminische Bildungsbürgertum. Zur Sozialgeschichte seiner Ideen*, Klaus Vondung, ed., Göttingen 1976, pp. 119–123.

11   Renzo De Felice, *Der Faschismus*, Stuttgart, 1977, pp. 47, 59.

my opinion, not correct. Speculations about the "new man" can be traced from racist ideologies of the Wilhelminian era well into the Third Reich. Collotti has already pointed out this oversight in his critique of Felice's book. But Collotti's objection, namely that it could be easily proved that the theme of the "new man" is "in its core a conservative mystification,"[12] is of course totally wrong. This symbol can be found in all progressivist, rationalist and other movements of the kind, from the Enlightenment up to Chinese communism. It should become obvious here that, despite all of the differences, there is a common trait of revolutionary ambition and probably also a common source for this state of mind. As to the difference between Fascism and National Socialism, I am of the opinion that it lies not in the revolutionary stimulus, but rather in the fact that the revolutionary traits of the latter underwent stronger ruptures and transformations, so that the outcome on the plane of politics and events looked quite different.

I have said that the ideological basis of National Socialism had already been established during the Wilhelminian era. After World War I this ideology was, if anything, further sharpened. Something else changed fundamentally because of the war and its effects. De Felice states that Fascism is not conceivable without the First World War, and the same is true for National Socialism. In World War I the German adherents of the "spiritual revolution" had still hoped the war would bring, in the manner of an apocalyptic event, the desired transformation of man and society. (I might mention in passing that the favorite symbol for the war was "last judgement" (*Weltgericht*).) When this transformation did not come, and when after the lost war the situation looked even worse than before, only one way seemed left for those not willing to adjust to reality. Something had to be done, and the impulse was given for magical action.

After this short historical survey, we now turn to a more systematic analysis of National Socialist magic and its revolutionary character. The structure of the way magic operates can be described as follows: (1) Magic begins with the belief that reality can be dominated if one finds the key to its mystery, the proper spell, or, to put it into more theoretical language, if reality can be constructed in such a way that it forms a coherent totality

12   E. Collotti, "Fascismo e nazional-socialismo," in *Fascismo e capitalismo*, N. Tranfaglia, ed., Milano 1976, p. 141.

that can be explained from one starting point. Therefore, Freud defined the "omnipotence of thoughts" as the principle of magic.[13] (2) Since reality resists being subjugated to such a mental construct, great efforts are necessary to manipulate and control consciousness so that disturbing elements can either be adjusted to the construct or kept outside. One can also describe these activities, as Robert Jay Lifton does, as "internal or psychological manipulations, "through which the attempt is made, "to achieve control over one's external environment."[14] (3) In consequence of the belief, to use Frazer's words, "that the control which they [i.e,, men] have, or seem to have, over their thoughts, permits them to exercise a corresponding control over things,"[15] action is taken in such a way that reality is made to seem as if it were in accord with the image one has conceived of it.

This formal description of magical procedure has to be completed with a description of its content. I subscribe to Eric Voegelin's definition of magic as the expansion of the will to power from the realm of phenomena to that of substance or the attempt to operate in the realm of substance pragmatically as if it were the realm of phenomena."[16] How does this content of magical manipulation manifest itself in National Socialism? My analysis will follow the steps of the description of magical procedure I have outlined above.

The one point from which the magic mind constructs the image of realty is "blood," conceived as the substantial basis of the *Volk*, on which the "new community" of the *Volksgemeinschaft* has to be built up. In the course of the nineteenth century the symbol of "blood" had more and more replaced *Volksgeist*, which had been a central symbol of the original "spiritual revolution." After World War I had destroyed everything which had been looked upon as manifestation of the *Volksgeist* (the power and the glory of the *Reich*, the supremacy of German *Kultur*, etc.), this substitution was

---

13   Sigmund Freud, "Animismus, Magie und Allmacht der Gedanken," in *Totem und Tabu*, Frankfurt – Hamburg, 1956, p. 97.

14   Robert Jay Lifton, *Revolutionary Immortality: Mao Tse-tung and the Chinese Cultural Revolution*, Harmondsworth, 1970, p. 38.

15   James George Frazer, *The Magic Art and the Evolution of Kings*, vol. I, 3rd edition, London, 1911, p. 420.

16   Eric Voegelin, *From Enlightenment to Revolution*, John H. Hallowell, ed., Durham 1975, p. 301.

finally completed. Hans Zöberlein, a leading National Socialist writer and a party official of high rank, summarized in his novel, *Der Befehl des Gewissens*, his feelings of the chaotic years after the war with the words: "The best and only thing we have left is Blood."[17] Human nature, its "substance" in the philosophical sense of the word, which is founded upon the tension toward the divine ground of reality beyond the realm of phenomena, is reduced to a phenomenal sector of reality, although the attempt is made to ascribe to this pseudo-substance the unchangeable quality of real substance. As Hitler himself expressed it: "Classes vanish, classes alter themselves, the destinies of men undergo changes, but something remains and must remain: the *Volk* as such, as the substance of flesh and blood."[18] "Good and pure blood" becomes the *summum bonum*, "the best and only thing we have left," of the phenomenal world; its antithesis, the anti-race of the Jews, is conceived as the *summum malum* and accordingly as an equally unchangeable substance. One of the most important propaganda films of the Third Reich had the title *The Eternal Jew*. The magic mind gathers everything that is against him and that opposes his image of reality into the idea of the "one and only enemy." This strategy led to the well-known obsession that there was, in Rosenberg's words, "a central operating plan of world Jewry," a "world conspiracy" between Jewish Bolshevism (the red international) and Jewish capitalism (the golden international).[19]

The psychic effort to bring and keep reality under control expresses itself in Hitler's permanent emphasis on his "absolute will," his "constant" or "never-changing will." Hardly any other word appears so often in his speeches and in his book *Mein Kampf*. Hitler's accentuation of the "will" is usually attributed to the influence of Schopenhauer and Nietzsche, but if such influences did exist, they were certainly watered down and vulgarized. It is unlikely that Hitler knew more than a few catch-words like the "will

17 Hans Zöberlein, *Der Befehl des Gewissens. Ein Roman aus den Wirren der Nachkriegszeit und der ersten Erhebung*, München, 1937, p. 298.
18 Adolf Hitler, Speech at Berlin, November 11, 1932, quoted from "Das dichterische Wort im Werk Adolf Hitlers," in *Wille und Macht*, Special Issue on the occasion of April 20, 1938.
19 Alfred Rosenberg, *Der entscheidende Weltkampf. Rede des Reichsleiters Alfred Rosenberg auf dem Parteikongress in Nürnberg 1936*, München, 1936, pp. 2, 4.

to power" through his own readings. The catch-words came in handy, however, to express his belief that a hard struggle was necessary to control consciousness so that a new image of reality could be constructed and in order to stress that he was the first and foremost to summon up the strength required to carry out this struggle: "From among the host of millions of men, who as individuals more or less clearly and definitely sense these truths or even grasp them, *one man* must step forward in order with apodictic force to form granite principles from the wavering world of the imaginings of the broad masses and to take up the struggle for the sole correctness of those principles, until from the shifting waves of a free world of ideas there rises up a brazen cliff of a united commitment in faith and will alike."[20]

The "will," as Hitler sees it, is the psychic power with which the magical consciousness is trying to construct and force through its image of reality, and it has therefore magical character itself. It is not to be compared with the will in the classical sense. I want to elucidate this problem by some further comments.

The will in the classical and Christian tradition is always and only the will ordered by reason. Cicero defined the will (*voluntas*) as the desire controlled by reason and set it clearly apart from concupiscence (*libido*) or unrestrained desire (*cupiditas effrenata*), "as to be found with every fool (*stultus*)."[21] This distinction (which was reiterated by Thomas Aquinas) leads to the first conclusion that the effort with which an irrational speculation is designed and pursued is in the proper sense no will at all, but nevertheless a strong existential power able to cause effects. It follows secondly that the person who exercises this kind of concupiscence is a fool (*stultus*) in the philosophical sense, for his choice of ends is not determined by reason. This does not mean, however, that at the same time the ends cannot be pursued with a high degree of practical intelligence. Furthermore, one is led to the question of means with which the uncontrolled "will" pursues its ends. Kant's analysis of the human will implies the answer to this question. It is relevant for an analysis of Hitler's "will," as J. P. Stern pointed out in his book on Hitler.

---

20 Adolf Hitler, *Mein Kampf*, vol. II, 7th edition, München, 1933, p. 419. Translation quoted from J. P. Stern, *loc. cit.*., p. 60.
21 Cicero, *Tuscul.* IV, p. 12.

Kant has shown that the human will is a disposition of the mind which, if adequate to reality, includes the consideration and choice of means appropriate or necessary for achieving the ends that the will is directed to: "He who wills an end, wills also (to the extent that reason has a decisive influence upon his actions) those indispensably necessary means that are in his power."[22] But if reason, which ought to be understood here again in the classical sense of the word, if reason, as in the magic mind, has no decisive influence, then the "will" is imagined as an absolute power that is sufficient in itself, i.e., it is believed that through the pure act of volition affects can be produced in external reality. When, for instance, Hitler in 1943 discussed with his generals the difficulty of transporting the division *Hermann Göring* from Sicily over to the mainland, in order to be prepared for the expected Allied invasion, he declared categorically: "It's not the ferries that are decisive. What is decisive is the will."[23]

To say that the magic mind separates itself from the means which in fact are necessary to attain its ends does not mean of course that the magic mind believes that something can be achieved in external reality without using the tools of external reality. Even the magician in "primitive" societies uses, in addition to his magic fertility rites, pragmatic means of irrigation and fertilization. But what is essential is his belief that these means work only because of the power of his magical operation. Similarly, to return to the example just mentioned, Hitler of course did not think that a division could be transported over the sea by a pure act of volition, but what he did think was that if the "will" was strong enough *some* means would be found; i.e., external reality would yield to the power of the mind.

The example shows the paramount role that is attributed to the manipulating power of consciousness, but it should not lead to the assumption that the matter rests there. On the contrary, along with his operation of mind, the modern "magician" also acts pragmatically. We have reached the

22 Immanuel Kant, *Grundlegung zur Metaphysik der Sitten*, sect. 2. *Kants gesammelte Schriften*, vol. IV, Berlin 1903, p. 417; translation quoted from J. P. Stern, *loc. cit.*, p. 71.

23 Walter Warlimont, *Im Hauptquartier der deutschen Wehrmacht 1939–1945. Grundlagen, Formen, Gestalten*, Frankfurt – Bonn 1964, p. 341; quoted from Werner Maser, *Adolf Hitler: Legende, Mythos, Wirklichkeit*, München – Esslingen 1971, p. 392.

point where the chief characteristic of National Socialist magic can be summed up in its conception of magical activity. This point might again cause some misunderstanding.

I want to stress once more that I do not intend to reduce the entire historical phenomenon of National Socialism to the person of Hitler and to blame all its deeds on him, by making him, instead of a "demon," the great "magician." When I use the term "magic" I mean something different from "demonism," and I hope that this distinction becomes clear in the course of my analysis of magic as a phenomenon of consciousness and the mode of action that it inspired. As to Hitler himself, it is obvious that he was not the only one with a magic mind. I quoted some other leading National Socialists above and could have added dozens more. And the story of Hitler's success shows that at least a considerable number of his followers were of a similar mind. What did distinguish Hitler from other leading National Socialists, to be sure, was his unrestrained concupiscence, his "absolute will."

Secondly, I do not contend of course that all actions of National Socialists or Hitler himself, not to mention those of the government of the Third Reich, can be interpreted as magical actions. What I intend to describe with the concept of magic is the driving impulse of a mode of consciousness and its working in *some* kinds of actions. Just because magic action *is* pragmatic action, clear distinctions cannot always be made. Actions can, however, be described as magical if they are undertaken in such a way that reality is made to conform to the inadequate image one has conceived of it and, with regard to the essence of the action, if one attempts to operate upon human nature as if it were a pragmatically manageable phenomenon. I want to demonstrate this concept in the realm of man and society. It is in this realm, also, that one can illustrate the revolutionary character of National Socialist magic, its debt to the "spiritual revolution" and its ultimate fulfillment.

First of all, I would like to recall some historical facts. Although the seizure of power by the National Socialists was no revolution in the sense of the French or Russian Revolution, German society underwent a process of considerable change between 1933 and 1945. Ralf Dahrendorf and David Schoenbaum were the first, to my knowledge, to point out that this process of change amounted to a "social revolution" whose content was "modernity."[24] Among the characteristics of this modernization, the most important, according to Dahrendorf and Schoenbaum, was a highly increased social mobility. The penetration of the whole of society and all its institutions by the National Socialist party and its numerous organizations, as well as the raising of a huge army, gave hundreds of thousands the unprecedented opportunity to improve, or at least to change, their status and profession, regardless of their former social background. Added to this vertical mobility was the increased horizontal mobility, ensured, among other institution and organizations, particularly by labor conscription (*Reichsarbeitsdienst*) and again by the army, which transferred people from one end of the country to the other. Although many National Socialist ideologists, and sometimes Hitler himself, subscribed verbally to values and ideas of a traditional social order, the importance and influences of many traditional social conditions and institutions, like the clearly separated classes, the independence of local and regional authorities, the churches and, last but not least, the family, were in fact diminished or neutralized by new organizations and institutions. As soon as Hitler had secured his power in 1934, he got rid of his conservative allies, and at about the same time, he reined in as well the "backward-freaks" ("*Rückwärtse*") of the *völkisch* groups in his movement.[25] It was not by mere accident that Rosenberg, the spokesman of the *völkisch* groups, even though he was allowed to maintain his belief that he was the party's chief ideologist, never achieved any real political influence. There is no doubt that Hitler himself thoroughly despised the "sclerotic old order" and did not care much about "tradition." When he declared his determination to build up a classless society of equal *Volksgenossen*, he meant it seriously to the extent that he attempted to permeate the whole society with his "will," to destroy all independent loyalties and influences, even private ones, and to organize society under the sole authority of the party so that it became manageable for his political purposes. The social changes thus set in motion partly resulted, no doubt, from the necessity to

24 Ralf Dahrendorf, *Gesellschaft und Demokratie in Deutschland*, München 1965, chapter 26; David Schoenbaum, *Hitler'Social Revolution: Class and Status in Nazi Germany 1933–1939*, Garden City, 1966.
25 Adolf Hitler, Speech at Nuremberg, November 5, 1934, quoted from *Reichstagung in Nürnberg 1934*, Berlin 1934.

seize, maintain, and extend power, and may have sometimes developed their own momentum beyond intention and control, but partly they were results of deliberate pragmatic actions of the magic mind.

Ideologically society was conceived as the "new community," as the classless *Volksgemeinschaft* in total equality, equal because of the common substance of blood. One kind of magic action in the realm of phenomena, corresponding with this belief, was the ritual actualization of that concept in the National Socialist cult. Scores of holidays, festivals and ceremonies were developed during the Third Reich, designed to commemorate Hitler's putsch of 1923 or his seizure of power in 1933, to celebrate events in the course of the year like Hitler's birthday, the first of May, solstice, harvest-festival, and even Christmas, in a National Socialist way, and finally to re-place Christian ceremonies in private life, such as baptisms, weddings and funerals, by National Socialist ceremonies. This cult was meant to perme-ate the mind, in public as in private life, with the new image of reality, to actualize this image again and again through ritual visualization, and to enable the participants in these ceremonies to believe that the image was *real*. One can show here that the National Socialist cult was not a dictato-rial measure of the lone magician Hitler, but that it responded to the psy-chic needs of many people of an equal mind. As early as 1928 Hanns Johst, a famous National Socialist writer and later president of the *Reichsschrif-tumskammer*, had expressed his desire for a new cult through which the soul could experience "in the community of equally minded, equally feel-ing, equally believing people the dream of salvation as displayed and en-visioned truth."[26] After 1933, the most impressive self-celebration of the "new community," as longed for by Johst, was the annual Party Congress in Nuremberg. At its main event, the nocturnal "hour of consecration" (*Weihestunde*) of the party functionaries, 240,000 people were massed to-gether in the *Zeppelin* stadium, underneath Speer's "dome of light," sur-rounded by tens of thousands of illuminated red swastika flags on the walls, and interspersed with 25,000 red and golden glittering standards which, all having been consecrated by Hitler's "blood banner" of 1923, symbolized total devotion as well as the unifying substance of the blood. What is essential is that in these ceremonies people underwent the psychic

26   Hanns Johst, *Ich glaube! Bekenntnisse*, München, 1928, p. 75.

and bodily experience that they were in fact all equal, formed one great community, the *Volksgemeinschaft*, and that they were left with this consciousness. Against this experience the inequalities that remained in everyday life seemed to be secondary.

But in addition, everyday life became penetrated and organized in such a way as to mobilize and equalize society under the rule of the party. There was hardly a way to extricate oneself from this effect. If one were not a member of the party or of one of its numerous organizations, from the *SA* down to the Association of National Socialist Women (*NS-Frauenschaft*), one probably was a member of the Association of Civil Servants (*Beamtenbund*) or the Association of Labor (*Deutsche Arbeitsfront*), both dominated by the party. If one did not participate in the cultural activities of the National Socialist *Kulturgemeinde*, one perhaps spent leisure time or vacation in one of the countless programs of the recreational organization *Kraft durch Freude*, and on top of that, one was permanently inundated by all sorts of activities, like the compulsory weekly Stew Day or the incessant collections of metal, paper or money. Above all, action was taken in a field in which a revolutionary structural change of society can be produced most effectively: in the field of education.

The National Socialist cult was also supposed to "form and create the New German man,"[27] but more important than ritual realization and affirmation, though these were certainly of high psychological significance, were of course the technical and organizational activities in education itself. In one of his talks with Hermann Rauschning, Hitler explained to what end he wanted to educate youth, and he disclosed in the process how his magic mind had reduced the nature of man to something phenomenal: "I want a violent, haughty, dauntless, cruel youth. . . The free and glorious beast of prey must gleam again through their eyes. Strong and beautiful I want my youth. I shall have them trained in all bodily exercises. I want an athletic youth. This is the first and most important. Thus I shall eradicate the thousands of years of human domestication. Thus I have the pure, noble material of nature at hand. Thus I can create the New. I don't want intellectual

---

27 "Entwicklung der Thingspielarbeit," in *Das Deutsche Volksspiel*, 1933/34, p. 172.

education. Thereby I would corrupt the youth through knowledge. . . [From this youth] springs up the man who is measure and center of the world, the creative man, the god-man."[28]

In 1938 Hitler made known in a public speech what kind of action had been taken and was further to be taken in order to achieve that aim. This speech revealed not only the magic essence of actions through which human nature was operated upon pragmatically as if it were something phenomenal, in accordance with the reduced image of the magic mind, but it also showed the revolutionary and quite "modern" character of the new education, which tended to cover the entire life of each member of society: "This youth certainly doesn't learn anything else than to think German and to act German, and when these boys at the age of ten come into our orga-nization and get and feel fresh air for the first time in their lives, then they come four years later from the *Jungvolk* into the Hitler Youth, and there we keep them again for four years. And then we are even less willing than before to return them into the hands of our old begetters of classes, but take them then immediately into the party, into the *Arbeitsfront*, into the *SA*, or into the *SS*, into the *NSKK* and so on. And when they are there for two years or one and a half years and shouldn't have yet become real Na-tional Socialists, then they go into the *Arbeitsdienst* and get drilled there again for six or seven months, all with one symbol, the German spade. And, after six or seven months, whatever should here or there still remain of class-consciousness or pride of place, then that is taken over for further treatment by the army for two years, and when they come back after two, three or four years, then we take them again immediately, so that by no means they have a relapse, into the *SA*, *SS*, and so on, and not one of them will be free again for his entire life."[29]

Just to round off the variety of magic actions, I want to point to some others through which an attempt was made to create the "new man" and

28 Hermann Rauschning, *Gespräche mit Hitler*, Zürich – New York, 1940, p. 237.
29 Adolf Hitler, Speech at Reichenberg, December 4, 1938; quoted from Her-mann Glaser, *Das Dritte Reich. Anspruch und Wirklichkeit*, 4th edition, Frei-burg i. Br. 1963, p. 114.

the "new society" in the realm of phenomena, or to defend them against the "one and only enemy": political measures "to protect race and state," such as the means to increase the birthrate of "valuable blood" on the one hand, and physical extermination of the Jews and other "worthless life" on the other; medical experiments in order to study the different modes of behavior and reaction of different races; plans for breeding human beings like cattle.

Magic action is pragmatic action in external reality. As such it can, though directed by a consciousness that comes short of grasping the substance of reality, indeed be successful as long as the means of external reality are at hand. If that is no longer the case, the magic character of consciousness is fully disclosed. The rational will, which combines consideration of ends as well as means, not to mention the necessity that means are governed by the rationality of the ends, will give up the pursuit of an end when the means are no longer there, or when they become inadequate. When toward the end of the war Hitler did not have tanks, airplanes and soldiers any longer, his "absolute will" was not diminished. He resorted to inadequate means like drawing up the "people in arms" (*Volkssturm*), or he plainly refused to concern himself with the question of means. And when the pressure of reality became so overwhelming that he could not evade it, he still stuck to the magic vision of reality, only its content got reversed: The German *Volk* had proved "to be the weaker one," he told Speer, "and the future will belong solely to the stronger eastern race (*Ostvolk*)," and consequently only one kind of action seemed to be left: "It is not necessary to take into consideration the basis which the people will need to continue a most primitive existence. On the contrary, it will be better to destroy these things, to destroy ourselves."[30]

---

30 Speer's evidence in court in Nuremberg, *Der Prozess gegen die Hauptkriegsverbrecher vor dem Internationalen Militärgerichtshof Nürnberg*, Nürnberg 1947–49, vol. XVI, p. 548.

National Socialism as a Political Religion: Potentials and Limits of an Analytical Concept[1]

After the fall of the communist regimes in Central and East Europe, a new interest has risen in comparing the dictatorships of the twentieth century. If one considers the new kind and quality of violent politics, represented by Italian Fascism, National Socialism, and Soviet Communism, and the historical role these regimes played in the twentieth century, the question suggests itself whether they shared common traits, despite their obvious differences. In order to grasp the essentially new and common features of these modern dictatorships, one has, in recent years, re-activated the concepts of 'totalitarianism' and 'political religion.' The concept of totalitarianism had been in eclipse somehow before 1989, especially in the 1970s, because of political and ideological reasons, but it is now being used again with less restraint in numerous publications and research projects. The concept of political religion has never had common acclaim in the past. Only in recent years has there been growing interest in this concept. The political scientist Hans Maier has conducted a large research project on totalitarianism and political religion.[2] The historian Markus Huttner has published an important book on the early history of the concepts of totalitarianism

---

1   Presented at the International Conference on "Political Religions as a Category of Contemporary History," University of Bern, 2003. First published in *Totalitarian Movements and Political Religions* Vol. 6/1 (June 2005).

2   *Totalitarismus und Politische Religionen. Konzepte des Diktaturvergleichs*, Hans Maier, ed., Paderborn, 1996; *Totalitarismus und Politische Religionen*, vol. II, Hans Maier and Michael Schäfer, eds., Paderborn, 1997; *Totalitarismus und Politische Religionen*, vol. III, *Deutungsgeschichte und Theorie*, Hans Maier, ed., Paderborn 2003.

and 'secular religion' in the 1920s and 1930s.[3] Eric Voegelin's seminal study of 1938, *Die politischen Religionen*, has been reprinted in German and translated into English.[4] A new journal, *Totalitarian Movements and Political Religions*, has been founded. Historians and scholars in the social sciences have published pertinent studies.[5] And, above all, Emilio Gentile has published two remarkable books on the sacralization of politics and on political religion, not only with respect to Italian Fascism, but of general significance.[6]

Nonetheless, the concept of political religion is still under dispute, and there are historians and social scientists who doubt that the concept has any analytical value. With respect to National Socialism, the subject matter of this article, the sceptics can be found, in particular, among the so-called 'structuralists' or 'functionalists,' for whom Hans Mommsen may serve as a representative.[7]

Scholars who subscribe to the analytical value of the concept of 'political religion' use it in order to capture characteristics of the totalitarian political movements and regimes of the twentieth century that, in their opinion, went beyond the analytical reach of traditional concepts such as despotism and tyranny. The concept of "political religion" has been meant,

3   Markus Huttner, *Totalitarismus und säkulare Religionen. Zur Frühgeschichte totalitarismuskritischer Begriffs und Theoriebildung in Großbritannien*, Bonn, 1999.

4   Eric Voegelin, *Die politischen Religionen*, Peter Opitz, ed., Munich, 1993; Eric Voegelin, *The Political Religions: The Collected Works of Eric Voegelin*, vol. 5; *Modernity Without Restraint*, Manfred Henningsen, ed., Colombia and London, 2000.

5   See, for instance, *Der Nationalsozialismus als politische Religion*, Michael Ley and Julius H. Schoeps, eds., Bodenheim, 1997; Claus-Ekkehard Bärsch, *Die politische Religion des Nationalsozialismus. Die religiöse Dimension der NS-Ideologie in den Schriften von Dietrich Eckart, Joseph Goebbels, Alfred Rosenberg und Adolf Hitler*, Munich, 1998; *Politische Religion? Politik, Religion und Anthropologie im Werk von Eric Voegelin*, Michael Ley, Heinrich Neisser, and Gilbert Weiss, eds., Munich 2003.

6   Emilio Gentile, *Il culto del littorio. La sacralizzazione della politica nell'Italia fascista*, Roma 2001; Ibid., *Le religioni della politica. Fra democrazie e totalitarismi*, Roma, 2001.

7   See Hans Mommsen, "Nationalsozialismus als politische Religion," in *Totalitarismus und Politische Religionen*, vol. II, pp. 173–181.

in particular, to define the essential meaning of "totalitarian," namely the claim of these regimes to dominate and control not only the political and social sphere, but all aspects of human existence, and secondly, to explain the outrageous and unprecedented use of violence against foreign enemies as well as against members of their own societies. With respect to National Socialism the concept of "political religion" is being considered even to provide an answer to the question of how the Holocaust could happen.

In what follows, I will test the analytical value and pertinence of the concept of political religion with respect to National Socialism in three steps: (1) I will point out "religious" elements in the area of organization and cult; (2) I will discuss the question whether there is something like an existential core of the National Socialist political religion; and (3) I will ask whether one can talk about a theology, eschatology, or apocalypse of the National Socialist religion.

Organization and Cult

National Socialism organized itself and presented itself in forms that bore resemblance to organizational and ritual forms of the Christian churches. This is a first and obvious reason for describing National Socialism as a political religion. The National Socialist party was organized in strict hierarchy from the onmnipotent *Führer* down to the last party member. Certain party organizations, especially the SS, resembled religious orders; so-called *Ordensburgen,* with their ceremonial halls (*Kulträume*), looked like secular monasteries. Special party offices developed and supervised scores of holidays, festivals, and ceremonies. These holidays and ceremonies formed a veritable cult that had resemblance to the Christian cult in several respects.[8] There were, first, numerous holidays spread over the year, in parallel to the canonical order of Christian holidays, beginning with January 30, designed to commemorate Hitler's seizure of power in 1933, and ending with winter solstice. There were, second, National Socialist ceremonies meant to replace the Christian ceremonies of baptism, wedding, and funeral. And there were, third, so-called 'morning celebrations' (*Morgenfeiern*) in parallel to Sunday services. Most of these ceremonies had prescribed liturgies that again resembled Christian ones. The same is true for particular

---

8   See my earlier work, *Magie und Manipulation. Ideologischer Kult und politische Religion des Nationalsozialismus,* Göttingen, 1971.

rituals like solemn processions or the adoration of relics, for instance of the so-called 'banner of blood' (*Blutfahne*) that had been carried at Hitler's putsch of 1923 and was shown to the public only twice a year.

Now, critics of the concept of political religion say that these traits have merely a formal character, that they are merely instrumental, in other words: propaganda. It is certainly true that the ceremonies mentioned above, party rallies and rituals, uniforms and banners, were meant to have a propagandistic effect, but this intention was not necessarily in conflict with the symbolic function of the ceremonies, rites, and relics. That is to say: the "forms" have to be taken seriously as symbolic expressions of something that indeed can be labeled as a political religion. Behind the forms there was faith.

Faith, or belief (*Glaube*), was a central and frequently used notion in the discourse of National Socialists. Hitler himself again and again spoke about his faith in Germany and in the German people and about the importance of this faith.[9] Other leading National Socialists referred to Hitler's faith and demanded of the Germans, especially of the party members, to unite in this faith.[10] The Nazi festivals and ceremonies were not only solemn demonstrations of the power and the glory of Hitler, his party and his regime, but provided ritual forms for confessions of faith.[11]

If one wants to analyze 'faith' under religious aspects, one has to do this in relation to its object. Otherwise one cannot grasp its particular character in comparison with attitudes of 'faith' in other religions. If one views National Socialism as a political religion, it is important to identify its articles of faith, its creed. Now, the liturgical texts and rites of the National Socialist cult offer plenty of material. In one of these texts, for instance, the assembly pronounces:

We believe in the blood . . .
We believe in the land . . .
We believe in the people . . .[12]

9   Adolf Hitler, *Mein Kampf*, 349th–351st ed. Munich,1938, pp. 416–419.
10   See my article, "'Gläubigkeit' im Nationalsozialismus," in *Totalitarismus und Politische Religionen*, vol. II, pp. 15–28.
11   K. Vondung, *Magie und Manipulation*, op. cit., pp. 117–121, 182, 189.
12   Eberhard Wolfgang Möller, *Die Verpflichtung*, Berlin, 1935, pp. 8, 10, 13.

In another text, built like a confession of faith and titled *The German Prayer*, we find the line:

We believe in our *Führer* . . .[13]

It seems that certain articles of what usually is labeled as the Nazi ideology can be identified as the articles of faith of the National Socialist political religion.

Again, the critics doubt its substance. Hans Mommsen stated: "The decisive objection to applying the theorem of 'political religion' to National Socialism is provoked by the fact that this theorem suggests an ideological conclusiveness and coherence that National Socialism—a sham phenomenon in every respect—never had."[14] We will see whether this criticism applies, whether it is at all to the point, when I now undertake the second step of my little investigation.

The Existential Core of the National Socialist Political Religion

It is Eric Voegelin's particular merit that in his book of 1938 he pointed out that National Socialism was not to be interpreted as a political religion simply because Nazis appropriated Christian linguistic symbols and ritual forms of the Christian church. The key reason why Voegelin understood National Socialism as a genuine religious phenomenon was that it had an existential core of religious character, which means that at its root lay religious experiences that led to the manifestation of a new faith. In Voegelin's words: "Wherever a reality discloses itself in the religious experience as sacred, it becomes the most real, a *realissimum*. This basic transformation from the natural to the divine results in a sacral and value-oriented recrystallization of reality around that aspect that has been recognized as being divine. Worlds of symbols, linguistic signs, and concepts arrange themselves around the sacred center; they firm up as systems, become filled with the spirit of religious agitation and fanatically defended as the "right" order of being.[15]

With respect to the *realissimum*, however, Voegelin made a basic distinction between "trans-worldly religions" (*überweltliche Religionen*), such as

13   Herbert Böhme, *Das deutsche Gebet*, Munich, 1936, p. 7.
14   *Totalitarismus und politische Religionen*, vol. 2, p. 181 (my translation).
15   E. Voegelin, *The Political Religions, Collected Works*, vol. 5, p. 32.

Judaism and Christianity, and "inner-worldly religions" (*innerweltliche Religionen*) "that find the divine in sub-contents of the world."[16] Given this distinction, it was possible to classify the religious elements manifest in National Socialism as being of the type of inner-worldly religions. The "sub-contents of the world," which the movement had elevated to the level of a *realissimum*, was the national community as a unit of common blood. Voegelin characterized the National Socialist national community as a "particular ecclesia" (as contrasted with the "universal ecclesia" proclaimed in Christianity), and as a "completely closed inner-worldly ecclesia" in which the community itself stood in place of God "as the source of legitimation of the collective person."[17] Among the symbols used by National Socialism to represent the "sacral substance" of the collective person or national community, Voegelin identified—alongside other terms drawn from the vocabulary of German Romanticism—that of the "national spirit" (*Volksgeist*). This spirit functioned as a *realissimum* lasting through the ages, "which becomes historical reality in individuals as members of their nation and in the works of such individuals." The "people in its plurality" becomes a national community, a "people in its unity," a "historical person, through the political organization." The organizer is the *Führer*; "the spirit of the people becomes reality in him and the will of the people is formed in him." Because the spirit of the people is an inner-worldly sacral substance, namely one that is tied to the blood, "the *Führer* becomes the speaker of the spirit of the people and the representative of the people because of his racial unity with the people."[18]

I have outlined Voegelin's interpretation in some detail to show how it incorporated a fundamental, anthropologically based definition of the term 'political religion.' For this understanding it is irrelevant that National Socialism did not have an elaborated and coherent ideology. What was important was the existential core and its unfolding into a particular set of articles of faith. The only criticism one could hold against Voegelin concerns his emphasis on the "spirit of the people" (*Volksgeist*). In my judgment, it played a much less important role for most Nazis than Voegelin assumed. Hitler himself almost always characterized the 'sacral substance' of the order

16 Ibid., pp. 32–33.
17 Ibid., p. 59, 64.
18 Ibid., pp. 65–66.

of being which he had proclaimed in a very direct manner. For example, in a speech shortly before he seized power, he declared: "Social rank passes away, classes change, human destinies are transformed, something remains and must remain with us: the people as such, as the substance of flesh and blood."[19] We can certainly rule out the possibility that Hitler had a sophisticated understanding of the theological or philosophical term 'substance'. However, the sense of the sentence quoted makes clear—and Hitler's eclectic vocabulary corroborates this—that he did understand the meaning of "substance" as something fundamental and primary, even as something absolute and divine, and that it was this which he sought to express. It also becomes clear that in this sentence the people in fact is elevated to the level of an inner-worldly *ecclesia*, which is founded upon the *realissimum* of common blood which remains constant through time.

The elevation of an inner-worldly entity to the level of a *realissimum* entails, as Voegelin established, a sacral and value-oriented recrystallization of reality and leads to the production of a large number of sacral symbols which congregate around the 'holy center'. This apparatus of symbols was presented, as I indicated, as articles of faith in the National Socialist ceremonies. Thus at the center of Nazi symbolism and creed stood the "Blood"; then came the "People" as the substantive bearer of the blood; the "Soil," the land, which nourishes the people; the "*Reich*," in which it finds its political realization; the "*Führer*" as the representative of the people and *Reich*; the "Flag" as the most holy material symbol. If one translates this apparatus back into the discourse of an ideology, the outcome indeed is neither very original nor intellectually demanding. But this is not the point. What was important was the plausibility of the creed, plausible because of its symbolic consistency and compelling because of its ritual manifestation at the ceremonies.

And yet, we can reconstruct additional areas of religious discourse, surrounding the existential core and showing a good deal of that coherence Hans Mommsen missed. The third step of my investigation leads to these areas of religious discourse.

---

19 Speech given by Hitler on 2 November 1932. Quoted from "Das dichterische Wort im Werk Adolf Hitlers" in *Wille und Macht*, 20 April 1938, n.p. (my translation).

Theology, Eschatology, Apocalypse

We can find religious vocabulary and, accordingly, religious interpretations of facts and events in different areas and situations, pronounced by politicians from Hitler down to simple *Ortsgruppenleiter* or *SA-Führer*, by writers of literature close to Nazi ideology, by literary critics and journalists, by university professors, schoolteachers, and other intellectuals who confessed to National Socialism. They contributed to the linguistic and symbolic part of the "political religion" phenomenon. We cannot expect, of course, to find something like an outspoken 'theology' of National Socialism as a political religion. In a particular area, however, we can reconstruct a system of thought that has structural and functional similarities with Christian theology. It is the area of National Socialist literature and literary criticism that is permeated, if not to say dominated, by religious discourse. I have shown this in detail a couple of years ago and therefore will restrict myself to the most important points.[20]

Most literary critics in the Third Reich, university professors as well as other authors who wrote about contemporary Nazi literature, interpreted these works as holy texts because they conveyed existential meaning to individuals, to society, even to history. The critics and scholars interpreted the authors of these holy texts as 'seers' and 'prophets,' and, for their part, they adopted in this scenario the role of theologians. Literary criticism became theology of literature.

The first part of Christian theology is biblical theology. The exegesis of the Old and New Testaments which uses hermeneutics as its major method is evaluated and systematized by a second part of Christian theology, systematic theology, whose results, primarily divided into dogmatics and ethics, form the basis for a third part, practical theology.

Similarly, Nazi theology of literature starts out by interpreting what is being presented as religious experiences. It is the religious discourse that makes the method of interpretation as used by literary critics and scholars appear as theological hermeneutics rather than hermeneutics as applied in

---

20 See my article, "Literaturwissenschaft als Literaturtheologie. Der religiöse Diskurs der Germanistik im Dritten Reich," in *Rhetorik*, vol. 16; *Rhetorik im Nationalsozialismus*, Joachim Dyck, Walter Jens, and Gert Ueding, eds., Tübingen, 1997, pp. 37–44.

literary criticism. The texts that are dealt with like holy scriptures seemingly convey the definite meaning of existence. As in systematic theology the meaning of the texts is divided into 'facts of faith' and 'moral laws.' The exposition of ethics marks the transition to practical theology. The field of action for practical theology is the religious community. Therefore it is quite logical that the Nazi theology of literature interprets the 'community of the people' (*Volksgemeinschaft*) as a community of faith (*Glaubensgemeinschaft*).[21] Literary criticism, as far as it adopts the role of practical theology, becomes a life science of the people (*volkhafte Lebenswissenschaft*),[22] i.e., a science that becomes practical and operates on society.

At this point, two remarks are in order. First, what I have outlined as a Nazi theology of literature was a product of intellectuals and not necessarily representative for a larger public. I will return to this reservation at the end of this article. Second, the Nazi theology of literature is a construct, resulting from a synthesis of diverse data of religious discourse. This is a methodological clarification that does not invalidate the result of the analysis. The same is true for what one could call a National Socialist eschatology.

In various ceremonies of the National Socialist cult certain historical events were presented as sacral events that together formed a 'history of salvation.'[23] The pivot of this history of salvation was Hitler's putsch of 9 November 1923. Although this putsch was a political disaster, Hitler interpreted it in retrospective as a 'sacral event,' especially in his speeches celebrating the occasion after 1933. The liturgical texts written for the yearly ceremonies had a similar consecrating effect. Hitler and the other authors interpreted 9 November 1923 as a sacral event because it had, in their eyes, a revelatory quality: it pointed to 30 January 1933. The death of sixteen of Hitler's followers in 1923 was interpreted as a sacrifice that was necessary as the condition for the subsequent victory. As a sacral event it was interpreted as a prefiguration, even anticipation, of the victory of 1933. In correspondence with the sacral event of 1923, Hitler's seizure of power was

---

21 Rudolf Bach, "Das Wesen des Sprech und Bewegungschores," in *Völkische Kultur*, 2 (1934), p. 213.
22 *Des deutschen Dichters Sendung in der Gegenwart*, Heinz Kindermann, ed., Leipzig, 1933, p. 10.
23 Cf. K. Vondung, *Magie und Manipulation*, pp. 85–87, 167–168, 180.

interpreted as a second sacral event which made true the revelation of 9 November. The content of this revelation was the *Reich* under National Socialist rule, for which commonly the chiliastic symbols of the "Third" or "Millennial" *Reich* were used. As an eternal *Reich*, it was considered to be the final period of the National Socialist "history of salvation."

The chiliastic symbols just mentioned lead me to the National Socialist apocalypse. I understand the apocalyptic worldview of Hitler and other Nazis as the most poignant manifestation of the National Socialist political religion and, above all, as the only plausible explanation for the Holocaust—if indeed an explanation in the sense of exposing motives and function is possible at all. I do not have the time here to show in detail the structural parallels and symbolic equivalences of the National Socialist apocalypse with the religious apocalyptic tradition,[24] therefore I will confine myself to the most prominent characteristics.

In *Mein Kampf* and in many of his speeches, Hitler developed an apocalyptic image of the world, in which he himself undoubtedly believed. He viewed world history as being determined by the struggle between two universal forces, whose irreconcilability he chiefly expressed in the dualistic symbolism of 'light-darkness,' and he believed the decisive battle to be close at hand, which would bring victory over the "deadly enemy of all light."[25] The 'power of evil' manifested itself for him in the Jews, the "evil enemy of mankind,"[26] onto whom he transferred the guilt for all material deficits of the world, as well as other imaginary dangers and threats. Hitler viewed the well-being of the entire world as being dependent on Germany's victory in the final apocalyptic struggle: "If our nation and our state becomes the victim of these bloodthirsty and avaricious Jewish tyrants of nations, the whole world will sink into the tentacles of this polyp; if Germany liberates itself from its clutches, this danger greatest for all nations will have been eliminated for the entire world."[27]

Other leading Nazis presented the same apocalyptic world-view. Goebbels noted in his diary: "The Jew is indeed the Antichrist of world

24 See my earlier work, *The Apocalypse in Germany*, Columbia and London, 2000.
25 Hitler, *Mein Kampf*, pp. 123, 216, 320, 421, 432, 724, 782, esp. pp. 346, 752 (my translation).
26 Ibid., p. 724 (my translation).
27 Ibid., p. 703 (my translation).

history."[28] Alfred Rosenberg also ascribed the role of the universal "evil enemy" to "World Jewry;" he assumed a "worldwide conspiracy" between Jewish capitalism and Jewish bolshevism against the "Nordic race of light." Rosenberg fomented a fear of universal destruction by producing a terrifying vision of "Jewish world revolution" and he prophesied an apocalyptic struggle, a "decisive world war (*ein entscheidender Weltkampf*)."[29] The same view was propagated by less known Nazis, by literature and film.

My understanding of this apocalyptic worldview as the most poignant manifestation of the National Socialist political religion and as an explanation of the Holocaust marks the extreme point of disagreement between supporters and opponents of the concept of political religion; it may be representative for objections in general and points to possible limits of the concept. We do not have Hitler's direct order, let alone a written order, for the large-scale murder of the Jews, with the exception perhaps of one document concerning the deportation of the French Jews.[30] It is even more difficult to prove a linkage between Hitler's apocalyptic worldview and the beliefs of Eichmann and other organizers of the Holocaust down to the perpetrators in the concentration camps. We will not get further than making the case plausible. But plausible it is, in my opinion, even to a high degree. The articles of faith of the National Socialist political religion were pronounced by Hitler himself and other leading Nazis, visualized and enacted in numerous celebrations, promulgated by 'believing intellectuals' of all sorts, from university professors to journalists and schoolteachers. Even if the 'believing intellectuals' were not necessarily identical with the perpetrators, even if the perpetrators were not themselves confident believers, the Nazi view of the world in its appearance as a political religion permeated the whole society, created a 'climate of opinion,' and provided the guidelines for behavior and action, provided even moral standards. And if one of the

28 *Das Tagebuch von Joseph Goebbels 1925–26*, Helmut Heiber, ed., 2nd ed., Stuttgart, 1960, p. 85 (my translation).
29 Alfred Rosenberg, "Der entscheidende Weltkampf," a speech by the Reichsleiter Alfred Rosenberg to the party congress in Nuremberg in 1936. Munich, n.d., pp. 2, 4 (my translation); ibid., *Der Mythus des 20. Jahrhunderts*, pp. 28, 590.
30 Geheime Reichssache, Vermerk, 10 Dec. 1942. American National Archives, Facsimile in *Frankfurter Allgemeine Zeitung*, 24 Jan. 2004, p. 33.

articles of faith said that the Jews were the "evil enemy of mankind" and that the survival and well-being of all good people depended on the destruction of that 'power of evil,' the implementation of this view was logical. Even for those who were not confident believers (and lacked other moral standards), this article provided at least a formal justification for their doings. In my opinion this explanation of the Holocaust is more plausible than Hans Mommsen's theorem of "cumulative radicalization."[31] There is no doubt, of course, that from the first measures of discrimination and persecution of Jews in 1933 up to the *Endlösung*, there was a process of radicalization and that external factors played a role in its course. But this process cannot explain its result, it cannot explain the decisive step from general antisemitism, even persecution, to organized mass-murder.

Now, the limits of the concept of political religion can, in general, be probably seen in the fact that its analytical grip does not reach beyond the evidence of demonstrated plausibility into the realm of matter-of-fact proof. In addition, and with respect to this realm of 'hard' facts, the concept of political religion certainly is not a panacea that could explain all aspects of National Socialism.

A final problem that also can be viewed as a limitation to the value of the concept is given by the term 'religion.' This means that by talking about National Socialism or other totalitarian ideologies and regimes as political religions one necessarily has in mind, as a measure and basis of comparison, the Christian religion, so that the National Socialist political religion could appear as a variant of the Christian religion, although a perverted one. It is true that some Christian theologians and pastors contributed to that perversion, but obviously there is a fundamental difference between the two 'religions' despite structural, formal, and symbolic similarities. We use the term 'religion' because of these similarities, and as long as we do not have a better concept we need it in order to point out the meaning and function of these similarities and, above all, the equivalences of the existential core of these modern phenomena.

---

31 Hans Mommsen, "Der Nationalsozialismus. Kumulative Radikalisierung und Selbstzerstörung des Regimes," in *Meyers Enzyklopädisches Lexikon*, Bd. 16. Mannheim 1976, pp. 785–790.

Are Political Religions and Civil Religions Secularizations of Traditional Religions?[1]

The concepts of "political religion" and "civil religion" originated in the eighteenth century in France and in the United States. At first, these terms were used indiscriminately in order to denote religious aspects of politics in a very general way. Jean-Jacques Rousseau argued in his *Contrat Social* (1762) that a well ordered society cannot do without a religion as its spiritual bond.[2] But he rejected Christianity because of several reasons and suggested a few simple dogmas as such a spiritual bond, namely the existence of God, belief in a life after death, reward of virtue and punishment of vice in the life to come, and tolerance. Rousseau suggested that these dogmas should be binding for all members of the society; he called them "civil religion" or "national religion."[3] The French philosopher Condorcet used the term "political religion" at the time of the French Revolution in a negative sense, for a system that forces citizens into a political creed that hinders them to use their independent reason.[4] In America, the writer, diplomat and politician Benjamin Franklin underlined the importance of religious faith for the social and political order; in 1749, even before the colonies

---

1   Presented at the International Conference on "Religions in Secular Societies in the Age of Globalization: Problems and Chances," Zhejiang University, Hangzhou, 2013.
    First published in *Review of Religions*. Vol. 1. Beijing: Press of Religious Culture, 2016.
2   Jean-Jacques Rousseau, *Du contrat social ou principes du droit politique*, Paris, 1960, pp. 327–336,
3   Ibid., p. 335.
4   Nicolas de Condorcet, "Laïcité et instruction publique. Premier Mémoire sur l'instruction publique" (1791–1792), http://action-republicaine.over-blog.com/article-14469260.html. Accessed on 08 August 2013.

declared their independence, he spoke of "the necessity of a public religion."[5] In the nineteenth century, president Abraham Lincoln called the Declaration of Independence and the Constitution of the United States the "political religion of the nation."[6]

In the twentieth century the meaning of the terms "political religion" and "civil religion" separated, and attempts were made to develop them into analytical concepts of political science and sociology. Among the authors who dealt with the notion of "political religion" as a new analytical concept the Viennese political scientist Eric Voegelin played a prominent role. In 1938, one month after Hitler's occupation of Austria, he published his book *The Political Religions*, in which he interpreted National Socialism as a political religion.[7] Before Voegelin, but with the same intention, Italian, Swiss, and English authors used the term "secular religion" for interpreting the totalitarian character of, first, Italian Fascism, then the Soviet regime under Stalin, finally National Socialism. Totalitarianism was itself a neologism; it was coined not only in order to designate the specific political system of dictatorial regimes, but especially with the purpose to point out that these regimes tried to be in control of all aspects of social life. The observation that totalitarian regimes even encroached upon the spiritual sphere of individuals and thus abolished the separation of the secular and the religious realm, led to the conclusion that totalitarian regimes themselves took on the character of a religion, of a secular or political religion. From then on, the term "political religion" was used predominantly for the religious features of totalitarian movements and regimes.

After the Second World War the concepts of political religion or secular religion did not, at first, play an important role in the analyses of National Socialism or other totalitarian regimes of the first half of the 20th century.

5 Benjamin Franklin, "Proposal Relating the Education of Youth in Pennsylvania" (1749); quoted in Emilio Gentile, *Politics as Religion*, Princeton and Oxford, 2006, p. 17.
6 Quoted in ibid., p. 2. Cf. Matthias Rüb, "Gottes Hand in Gettysburg," in *Frankfurter Allgemeine Zeitung*. 08 July 2013, p. 7.
7 Erich Voegelin, *Die politischen Religionen*, Schriftenreihe "Ausblicke," Wien 1938. Only a few copies were sold. The publisher, Bermann-Fischer, emigrated to Stockholm, and a second edition of Voegelin's book was published there in 1939.

This changed in the nineties. Voegelin's book *The Political Religions* was republished in a new edition and translated into English, French and Italian. German as well as American, British, Swiss, and Italian historians and political scientists discussed afresh the concept in numerous conferences and publications. In the year 2000 a journal was founded, dedicated to the investigation of *Totalitarian Movements and Political Religions*, as the title of the journal indicated. In recent years the Italian historian Emilio Gentile has systematized the discussion of the concept in two books and numerous articles.[8]

The term "civil religion" has first been advanced to an analytical concept by the American sociologist Robert N. Bellah in his article "Civil Religion in America," published in 1967.[9] As the title of Bellah's article shows, the United States was the model for his clarification und definition of what a "civil religion" would be. In short, Bellah defined the American civil religion as "an institutionalized collection of sacred beliefs about the American nation." Bellah and other scholars in his footsteps presented a detailed collection of beliefs and rituals that originated in the American Revolution. The Declaration of Independence, the Constitution and the Bill of Rights forged the connection between American patriotism, especially the idea of republican liberty and civil rights, and religion. The God who was invoked in the Declaration of Independence and whom all presidents of the United States address in every speech, as well as sportsmen and pop-stars and even the one-dollar bill, this God is not the God of a particular denomination.

---

8   For the history of the concepts of secular and political religions, see Markus Huttner, *Totalitarismus und säkulare Religionen. Zur Frühgeschichte totalitarismuskritischer Begriffs und Theoriebildung in Großbritannien*, Bonn 1999; Emilio Gentile, *Le religioni della politica: Fra democrazie e totalitarismi*, Roma and Bari, 2001; English translation *Politics as Religion*, Princeton and Oxford, 2006, esp. pp. 1-4; ibid., "Political Religion: A Concept and its Critics – A Critical Survey," in *Totalitarian Movements and Political Religions*, Vol. 6, No. 1 (2005), esp. pp. 25–28; see also, Klaus Vondung, *Deutsche Wege zur Erlösung. Formen des Religiösen im Nationalsozialismus*, München, 2013. See the chapter "Politische Religion?" pp. 23–35.

9   Robert N. Bellah, "Civil Religion in America," *Daedalus. Journal oft the American Academy of Arts and Sciences*, Vol. 96.1 (1967), pp. 1–21. - Robert N. Bellah died on 30 July 2013 at the age of 86 in Berkeley.

Originally this God was protestant, but meanwhile Catholics and Jews, even Muslims, can identify this God with the God of their own belief.[10]

In Germany of today, as well as in other European countries, the concept of civil religion is less applicable than in the United States. The first nineteen articles of the German constitution list the general human rights and the basic civil rights of the German citizens; there is no reference to God or to religious standards. In the preamble to the constitution, however, the authors of the constitution, speaking for the entire German people, confess to a "responsibility to God."[11] In Europe, one can observe a similar uncertainty with respect to the relationship between the political order and religious values. Before the Treaty of Lisbon on the European Union was signed in 2007 there was a heated discussion whether there should be a reference to God in the preamble. Some countries like Spain or Ireland were for it; others, like France, where a strict separation exists between state and church, were against it. Finally, the majority of European countries decided against a reference to God. But: In the preamble to the treaty the European states solemnly declare that they draw from the cultural, religious and humanistic heritage of Europe, from which developed the imprescriptible (invulnerable) and inalienable rights of the human being as well as freedom, democracy, equality and the rule of law as universal values.[12] Believing Christians maintain that these values would not have developed without the Christian image of the human being as the image of God (lat. *imago dei*) and Christian morality.

But now let me approach the question that I have chosen as a guideline for my deliberations: Are political religions and civil religions secularizations of traditional religions? After my preliminary remarks about political religions and civil religions in Europe and in the United States I can, at first, specify this question. It has become clear that the matter of comparison, the religion that perhaps or supposedly was secularized, is not any

---

10 The memorial service at the Washington Cathedral after 9/11 was attended by pastors and priests, rabbis and mullahs of all these religions and denominations.

11 *Grundgesetz mit Menschenrechtskonvention etc*, Udo Di Fabio, ed., 43rd edition, München, 2011, p. 1.

12 Ibid., p. 205, cf. p. 367.

traditional religion, but specifically the Christian religion. The correct reading of the question therefore should be: Are political religions and civil religions, as we observe them in Europe and the United States, secularizations of the Christian religion? Secondly: What does secularization of the Christian religion mean, in general and in particular with respect to the concepts of political religion and civil religion?

Secularization is a Western concept that needs explanation, although I have to confine myself to a few points that are necessary for my argument.[13] Basically secularization means: Turning something that belongs to the sacred sphere to the secular sphere. Originally secularization in this basic sense was a legal concept in Christian countries in Europe. It meant: Turning property that belonged to the church or to monasteries into the hands of worldly powers, into the hands of the "state." This process began after the Thirty Years War, which ended in 1648, continued throughout the eighteenth century and reached its peak during the Napoleonic era, in the beginning of the nineteenth century. During the same period of time a more general understanding of secularization evolved, namely secularization just as the "decrease of religion."

In addition to this general understanding and to the legal concept, a more sophisticated understanding of secularization evolved, beginning in the eighteenth century and fully developing in the nineteenth and twentieth centuries: The concept of secularization was transferred from the legal sphere to philosophy, to the history of ideas, to politics. This means that certain phenomena in modern European history, especially propositions on the course and the goal of history, i.e., theories or philosophies of history, were considered to be secularizations of theological concepts. Accordingly, progressivism of the 18th century and other philosophies of progress, also Marxism and other theories of history, were considered to be secularizations of Christian eschatology. The Christian idea of a salvation history, especially

---

13   Cf. Hans Blumenberg, *Säkularisierung und Selbstbehauptung*, Frankfurt a. M. 1974; Hermann Lübbe, *Säkularisierung. Geschichte eines ideenpolitischen Begriffs*, Freiburg and München, 2nd ed. 1975; *Säkularisierung*, Heinz Horst Schrey, ed., Darmstadt, 1981; *Religion und Gesellschaft. Texte zur Religionssoziologie*, Karl Gabriel, ed., Paderborn, 2004; Jürgen Habermas and Joseph Ratzinger, *Dialektik der Säkularisierung. Über Vernunft und Religion*, Freiburg i. Br., 2005; Charles Taylor, *Ein säkulares Zeitalter*. Frankfurt, 2009.

Joachim of Fiore's theory of three phases of spiritual fulfillment in history as well as apocalyptic prophecies, were interpreted as models for secular speculations. Representatives of such interpretations were the writer and philosopher Gotthold Ephraim Lessing in the eighteenth century, in the nineteenth and early twentieth centuries Wilhelm Dilthey and Ernst Troeltsch, and after 1945 Karl Löwith and others.[14]

Now, do these usages of the notion "secularization," of the legal concept of secularization or of the philosophical concept, apply to the notions of political religion and civil religion? Obviously not. We do not have a transformation of the sacred to the secular, but quite the contrary. What we do observe is the *sacralization* of essentially secular, namely political and ideological matters.[15] This is true for political as well as civil religions. I am choosing again the National Socialist political religion and the American civil religion as conspicuous examples and I restrict myself to a few pertinent points.

In either case we have founding myths that transform certain historical events into "holy stories." For the American myth the most important event in a series of others took place on April 19, 1775, when in Lexington, Massachusetts, the first shots of the American revolution were fired, shots that – according to the myth – "were heard around the world."[16] In the case of National Socialism, the story of Hitler's putsch on November 9, 1923, was told as a holy myth. Although the putsch failed and left sixteen of Hitler's followers dead on the steps of the *Feldherrnhalle* in Munich, this disaster

---

14 Gotthold Ephraim Lessing, "Die Erziehung des Menschengeschlechts" (1780), in *Lessings Werke*, newly edited by Franz Bornmüller, 5 vols. Leipzig n. d., vol. 5, esp. p. 615; Ernst Troeltsch, "Über das Wiedererwachen der Geschichtsphilosophie," *Gesammelte Schriften*, Tübingen 1922, vol. 3, p. 57; Wilhelm Dilthey, "Einleitung in die Geisteswissenschaften," *Gesammelte Schriften*, 5th and following editions, Stuttgart and Göttingen, 1962 sq.; Karl Löwith, *Weltgeschichte und Heilsgeschehen. Die theologischen Voraussetzungen der Geschichtsphilosophie* (1953), Stuttgart 4th ed., 1961.

15 Cf. *The Sacred in Twentieth-Century Politics. Essays in Honour of Professor Stanley G. Payne*, Roger Griffin, Robert Mallett, John Tortorice, Houndmills Basingstroke, eds., 2008, esp. chapter "The Sacralization of Politics."

16 This is the inscription on the memorial monument by the side of the bridge to Concord where the skirmish continued.

was considered to be a sacred event that anticipated Hitler's victory in 1933. The Nazis who had been killed in 1923 were venerated as martyrs, the *Feldherrnhalle* as a sacred place, November 9 became a sacred holiday in the Third Reich.[17] The American founding myth knows martyrs, too, for instance the martyrs of the so-called Boston Massacre, holy places like the common at Lexington or Valley Forge, and it led to the institution of a sacred holiday, the 4th of July.

In addition, the political religion of National Socialism and the American civil religion encompass such things as the quasi-religious veneration of political leaders, in the Nazi case of Hitler himself, in America of past political leaders like Washington, Jefferson or Lincoln. There are holy scriptures, Hitler's *Mein Kampf*, in the United States the Declaration of Independence, the Constitution and the Bill of Rights. There are rituals of religious character and political symbols like flags considered to be sacred.

These are similarities. Of course there are differences in *content* that justify the distinction between political religion and civil religion. The American civil religion sacralizes, in reference to a God who originally was thought to be the Christian God, not only patriotic values and civil rights, but also fundamental human rights as they had been pronounced in the Declaration of Independence, in the Constitution and the Bill of Rights.[18] To a lesser degree, lesser with respect to the degree of sacralization, the catalogues of human and civil rights in the German Constitution as well as in the Treaty of Lisbon can be seen—considering the references to God or the European religious heritage in the preambles of these documents. By contrast, the National Socialist political religion sacralized the Aryan race and the pure-blooded community of the German people; this sacralization served as a justification for the persecution and extermination of the Jews and other peoples that were considered to be inferior to the German people. In addition, the sacralization of the *Führer* as the infallible supreme political

---

17   For a detailed account of the Nazi myth of November 9, see K. Vondung, *Deutsche Wege zur Erlösung*, pp. 65–79.

18   Especially the following sentence in the Declaration of Independence: "We hold these truths to be *self-evident, that all men are created equal,* that they are endowed by their *Creator* with certain *unalienable Rights,* that among these are *Life, Liberty and the pursuit of Happiness.*" Emphasis my own.

authority led to the abolishment of all civil rights.[19] The conclusion is obvious that a civil religion is more humane and democratic than a political religion of the Nazi type. Nonetheless one can ask whether a civil religion is at all necessary for a well- ordered democratic society, as Rousseau had argued, and whether a civil religion might become dangerous, too, under certain circumstances.

This question induces me to a final consideration and brings me back to the observation that political as well as civil religions are not secularizations of the Christian religion but are sacralizations. On second glance, however, political and civil religions indirectly have something to do with the process of secularization. In the Middle Ages the political and spiritual order were combined in the idea of the "holy empire," in Latin: the *sacrum imperium*.[20] In the seventeenth and eighteenth centuries the *sacrum imperium* had its actual end; this means: in political theory and in national law, church and state were dissociated. The concepts of politics and religion for two separate spheres followed this dissociation.[21] The legal concept of "secularization" ran parallel to this development, as well as, a little later, the philosophical concept. In consequence, the political sphere threatened to become spiritually void. Thus the spiritual void was gradually filled by ways of sacralizing secular, political matters. Therefore one could conclude that the process of secularization in European early modernity was a precondition for the sacralization we observe in political and civil religions.

---

19 For more detailed information about the connection between the sacralization of race and the Führer in National Socialism and the Holocaust, see K. Vondung, *Deutsche Wege zur Erlösung*, pp.119–137.

20 Cf. Alois Dempf, *Sacrum Imperium. Geschichts und Staatsphilosophie des Mittelalters und der politischen Renaissance,* München and Berlin, 1929; 3rd ed. Darmstadt 1962.

21 Cf. E. Voegelin, *Die politischen Religionen,* op. cit., p. 9.

On Eric Voegelin

Eric Voegelin, the Crisis of Western Civilization, and the Apocalypse[1]

The last two volumes of *Order and History*, as the series was planned originally, were meant to treat "the modern national states, and the development of Gnosis as the symbolic form of order"; the final volume was to bear the title *The Crisis of Western Civilization*.[2] As we all know, Eric Voegelin broke with the original program in 1974 with *The Ecumenic Age* as the new volume 4. The Gnosticism thesis, although not abandoned expressly, lost some weight. The final volume of *Order and History*, as projected then and published as a posthumous fragment, bore the title *In Search of Order*, thus shifting the accent from the negative to the positive, as it were, from the presentation and analysis of the disorder of the modern age, the "Crisis of Western Civilization," to the existential quest for truth concerning the order of being.

The break with the original concept of *Order and History* had two main reasons, as Voegelin outlined in the preface to *The Ecumenic Age*. First, Voegelin had become aware of and had to take into account that "the important lines of meaning in history . . . did not run along lines of time."[3] He

1   Presented at the International Conference on "Voegelin's Vision of Order and the Crisis of Civilization in the Twentieth Century," University of Manchester, 1994.

    First published in *International and Interdisciplinary Perspectives on Eric Voegelin*, Stephen A. McKnight and Geoffrey L. Price, eds., Columbia and London: University of Missouri Press, 1997.

2   Eric Voegelin, Preface to *Israel and Revelation, Order and History*, vol. 1, Baton Rouge 1956, p. X.

3   Erid Voegelin, *The Ecumenic Age, Order and History*, vol. 4, Baton Rouge 1974, p. 2.

concluded: "The process of history, and such order as can be discerned in it, is not a story to be told from the beginning to its happy, or unhappy, end."[4]

The original program of Order and History suggested a rather unhappy end: the Gnostic disorder of modernity. But the insight that the process of history is not a story to be told from the beginning to the end, but "a mystery in process of revelation," ruled out not only the tale of a consecutive sequence of differentiations but also the respective tale of the pertinent deformations.[5] Deformation of differentiations, Voegelin stated, "is a force in world history of the same magnitude as differentiation itself."[6] The obvious conclusion is that it does not run along lines of time any more than the process of differentiation.

The second reason for the break with the original concept of *Order and History* was a material one. With respect to the disordering forces in history, the concept of *Order and History*, as outlined in the preface to volume 1, reflected a stand that Voegelin had developed while working on the *History of Political Ideas* and that he brought to the fore in *The New Science of Politics*: that the nature of modernity is Gnosticism. Although derived, of course, from antique Gnosticism, Voegelin turned the notion of Gnosticism, or *Gnosis*, when applied to modern ideologies or political movements, into a very comprehensive critical concept. In Voegelin's view the Gnostic speculator feels totally alienated in this world because he is convinced that he belongs to a reality beyond the given world. The core of Gnosticism is the striving for self-redemption through knowledge – Gnosis. As *The History of Political Ideas* shows, as well as *The New Science of Politics* and *Science, Politics, and Gnosticism*, Voegelin's concept of modern Gnosticism comprised as many and various phenomena as the Anabaptists of the sixteenth century, the English Puritans of the sixteenth and seventeenth centuries, the philosophies of Hegel and Marx, Marxism, National Socialism, and Stalinism.[7]

---

4   Ibid., p. 6.
5   Ibid.
6   Ibid., p. 38.
7   A pertinent chapter of the unpublished *History of Political Ideas* was published recently in German translation in *Das Volks Gottes: Sektenbewegungen und der Geist der Moderne*, Peter J. Opitz, ed., Munich 1994.

Voegelin was heavily attacked for his Gnosticism thesis. It did, as a matter of fact, and as I mentioned before, lose weight in his later work. The reason was not the criticism against it; Voegelin certainly maintained the critical thrust of his thesis, especially with respect to its essential core, as the introduction to *The Ecumenic Age* shows.[8] But the differentiation of his philosophy of history, which led to the break of the original concept of *Order and History*, also led, I think, to a differentiated view of deformations. Although the Gnosticism thesis could be maintained with respect to its essential core, it seemed to be necessary, with respect to the historical phenomena, to distinguish, for instance, Hermeticism from Gnosticism, and, above all, Apocalypticism, as expressed in Jewish and Christian visions and in Millenarian, Chiliastic, and Messianic movements. Quite a few of the phenomena that Voegelin had dealt with under the heading of Gnosticism in the unpublished *History of Political Ideas* and in *The New Science of Politics* are usually attributed, as one knows, to the apocalyptic tradition.

As early as the 1960s, Voegelin had also begun to differentiate deformations of differentiations within the context of the philosophy of history. In 1964, at the University of Munich, he taught a graduate seminar on "Philosophy of History," subtitled "History and Apocalypse," which covered the Book of Daniel, the Revelation of John, and apocryphal apocalyptic texts, as well as the writings of Otto of Freising, Kant, Condorcet, Novalis, and Marx. Ten years later, in *The Ecumenic Age*, "apocalyptic and Gnostic movements" are mentioned as disordering forces of equal importance in modernity.[9] With respect to antiquity, the "syncretistic spiritualism" of Gnosticism is "placed as a symbolism of resistance by the side of the apocalyptic development in Judaism."[10] In certain aspects the Jewish apocalypse, interpreted as a deviation of prophetic pneumatism, can even be viewed as a forerunner of Gnosticism in the deformed pneumatic process.[11]

---

8   E. Voegelin, *The Ecumenic Age*, op. cit., pp. 20–27.
9   Ibid., p. 48.
10   Ibid., p. 24.
11   Ibid., pp. 26–27. It is interesting that the same relationship between Apocalypticism and Gnosticism can be detected in modernity. Ernst Bloch, for instance, starts out, in his *Geist der Utopie* and *Thomas Münzer als Theologe der Revolution*, with apocalyptic speculations that in his *Das Prinzip Hoffnung* flow into Gnosticism; see my analysis of Bloch in my book *Die Apokalypse in*

However the relationship between Gnosticism and Apocalypticism may be viewed at different historical times, Voegelin made it clear in *The Ecumenic Age* that the process of pneumatic differentiation has a counterpart in the differentiation of deformations, and these also have to be distinguished and analyzed. This is not an easy task, however: "Deformations of symbols already differentiated are indeed more difficult to understand than the original symbols themselves, because as a rule the deformers neither analyze their method of deformation themselves, nor are they informative about their motives. And yet, the work of penetration must be done because deformation of differentiations achieved is a force in world history of the same magnitude as differentiation itself."[12]

In 1964, I had the chance to attend Voegelin's graduate seminar on "History of Philosophy—History and Apocalypse," and to deliver a paper on chapters 2 and 7 of the Book of Daniel without knowing at that time that this seminar would be the stimulus for a long-lasting preoccupation with Apocalypticism that, twenty-four years later, finally led to my publication of a comprehensive study of the apocalyptic tradition in Germany.[13] I had become aware that apocalyptic speculations and apocalyptic movements played a paramount role in German history, in my opinion more important than Gnosticism in its more limited sense. Moreover, modern Apocalypticism launched an even more radical attack against reality than Gnosticism, an evaluation, by the way, that Voegelin seemed to share, with respect to antiquity, when he spoke of the "apocalyptic desire to destroy

---

Deutschland (Munich 1988, pp. 225–257, 452–462). A similar constellation can be found in Ernst Jünger's work; I have interpreted Jünger's early speculation on history as apocalyptic (*Die Apokalypse in Deutschland*, pp. 382–390, 476–479). The philosopher Peter Koslowski views Jünger's later work as Gnostic (see his book *Der Mythos der Moderne. Die dichterische Philosophie Ernst Jüngers*, Munich, 1991). Our respective papers at an international conference on Jünger at the Sorbonne, Paris, in 1995, complemented each other strikingly (*Etudes Germaniques*, Paris, 1996). This complex issue begs further investigation.

12 E. Voegelin, *The Ecumenic Age*, op. cit., p. 38.

13 K. Vondung, *Die Apokalypse in Deutschland*. An English translation was published by The University of Missouri Press: *The Apocalypse in Germany*, Columbia and London, 2000.

the cosmos itself."[14] What is more, I was challenged by Voegelin's call to penetrate the deformations of differentiated symbols, especially since he himself, in his late years, understandably paid more attention to the process of pneumatic differentiation than to its deformation.

In what follows I will give a necessarily abbreviated description of apocalyptic symbolism and an analysis of its relationship to experiences of crisis including a discussion of some theoretical and methodological problems pertaining to the question of how experiences of crisis and their symbolization are to be adequately analyzed. Voegelin's investigation will be the basis and point of departure for my own attempts to carry further the analysis of the apocalyptic symbolism. I will briefly sketch the scope of the issues and problems involved. First, when I refer to the subject matter of *crisis*, I do not mean crisis as an objective, given fact (which does not exist), but rather the consciousness of crisis as expressed in literature, philosophy, political writings, and other sources. Nonetheless, one can talk about crisis as a socio-historical phenomenon in our century since consciousness of crisis has been expressed almost constantly, although with different content and coloring at different stages. The consciousness of crisis of particular individuals has formed, in Voegelin's words, a "social field of consciousness."[15] Within this field there is again a particular and very typical form in which the consciousness of crisis has been expressed, and this form can be called "apocalyptic." The apocalyptic variety can be found in German sources in philosophy and in *fin de siècle* literature; in poems, sermons, and political writings of World War I; in Expressionist literature; in philosophy and literature between the wars; in National Socialism; and, after 1945, in the self-interpretations of the former Germen Democratic Republic; the West German terrorist gang "Red Army Faction"; and, more recently, in warnings against the devastation of the world as a result of industrial progress, or in the "end-of-history" concepts of postmodernism.

The social field of consciousness that reflects crisis and that can be viewed as a socio-historical phenomenon is rooted in the consciousness of individuals. The individual consciousness of crisis is also an existential

14 E. Voegelin, *The Ecumenic Age*, op. cit., p. 10.
15 E. Voegelin, *Anamnesis: Zur Theorie der Geschichte und Politik*, Munich, 1966, pp. 340–346.

phenomenon; it can be viewed as the expression of the existential crisis of particular individuals. If I single out the form of expression that I am calling *apocalyptic*, the question arises as to how the existential and socio-historical phenomena are connected. This question pertains not only to the subject matter, but also, at the same time, to theoretical and methodological problems, and consequently leads to additional questions. If I understand the apocalyptic expression of crisis as being rooted in the consciousness of individuals, I have to ask, with respect to the subject matter, whether there is a particular type of apocalyptic experience that serves as the motive for apocalyptic expressions of crisis. This question implies the additional one: whether there is something constant in apocalyptic expressions of crisis or in the respective motivating experiences that would permit us to call phenomena of the twentieth century *apocalyptic* at all (if we use this term as a typological one for otherwise historically contingent phenomena). With respect to theory and method I have to ask: how can one say something about experiences by analyzing verbal expressions?

To amplify the problems and questions sketched above, with respect to the apocalyptic type of crisis, let me first give a *typological* description of what the apocalypse is, although this seems to partly prejudge the question raised above. The apocalypse originates in situations in which people feel endangered and humiliated, oppressed and persecuted in their entire existence: spiritually, politically, socially (whether this feeling is justified or not). They interpret their experiences of suffering in such a way that the world in which they live seems to be void of meaning, utterly corrupt and evil. They long for salvation, but they do not believe that by partial improvements or reforms anything decisive could be achieved. Salvation, they believe, can be achieved only if the old corrupt world perishes and the "evil enemy," who is guilty of the corruption, is destroyed. They understand this situation not only as a crisis, but look upon this crisis as being universal and imminent. They consider the final decision as being inescapable and within sight. Thus, the apocalypse is characterized, first, by a strict dualism, that is, by a radical division between the corrupt old world and the perfect future one; between the "evil enemy" and the chosen, who still suffer now, but soon will triumph. Second, it is characterized by the conviction that salvation must be preceded by the devastation of the old world and the destruction of the "evil enemy." These additional characteristics usually follow:

the pertinacity and the universalism of the apocalypse, as well as the expectation of imminence.

The specifics of the apocalypse are verbally expressed in dramatic visions of the imminent decision as a final terrible battle. The destruction of the old world is depicted most often in images of devastating powers of nature—— flood, storm, fire, and earthquakes. The strict dualism of the apocalypse, the division between the deficient old world and the expected new condition, which is also a moral separation, expresses itself in images of filth and purity, illness and sanity, darkness and light. The "evil enemy" is depicted as a cruel, malicious, repulsive, and loathsome beast. The expected change of reality and of the entirety of existence is expressed in symbols like "transformation," "regeneration," "renovation," "salvation," "redemption," and "resurrection." Words expressing the absolute like "all" and "everything," "the whole" and "the last," represent the pertinacity of the apocalypse.

The apocalyptic expressions of crisis, as we find them in twentieth-century Germany, are descendants of the Judeo-Christian apocalyptic tradition, although some decisive differences have to be marked. First, in the Judeo-Christian apocalypses, the destruction of the old world and the transformation of reality is brought about by God himself, whereas in the modern apocalypse this task is ascribed to men. Second, in the latter, the state of salvation is envisioned not as a "heavenly Jerusalem," but as a "paradise on earth." However, with respect to structure, motivation, images, and symbols, the modern apocalypse is so closely related to the Judeo-Christian one, that it is justified to use the term *apocalypse* to designate these expressions of crisis.

There is a tension between *apocalypse* as a socio-historical phenomenon and *apocalypse* as the expression of an existential crisis. The apocalypse has to do with history. It interprets history in a particular way and therefore presupposes a consciousness of history. This is shown already by the earliest apocalyptic texts in the Book of Daniel. It is true that the consciousness of history in old Israel cannot be compared with the modern one. There is no Hebrew word in the Old Testament, for example, that would correspond to our word *history*. Nevertheless the scriptures of the Old Testament give evidence that there was from the time of Moses and the Exodus a conception of history as a process influenced by God. This conception solidified gradually and became what is called the concept of "salvational history;" that is, history as a chain of events, directed by God, from creation to salvation. The origins of the apocalypse are characterized by a tension toward salvational history. In Israel, the apocalyptic symbolism originated between the second Babylonian Exile and the reign of the Seleucids over Palestine when belief in salvational history was radically disappointed. Voegelin marked this point: "The succession of empires is senseless; there is no hope of pragmatic victory over the imperial enemy or of a spiritual transformation of mankind. Since the present structure of reality is without meaning, a divine intervention has to change the structure itself, if divine order is to be reintroduced. The consciousness of the divine ordering reality has contracted into the visions of an apocalyptic thinker."[16]

The ancient apocalyptic conception of history, then, presupposes the concept of a salvational history as its foil. The same is true for modernity. In the modern form the concept of salvational history is replaced by concepts of history that differ in content, but are similar in structure, namely by concepts of history as a systematic process of progress. In any case, the apocalyptic conception of history presupposes that history possesses a quality that in modern language would be called *meaning*. The apocalyptic responses to the experience of history void of meaning are plausible only on this assumption.

The previous observations imply that the apocalypse is not an archetype, but a historically contingent phenomenon that originated at a certain historical point within a particular political, social, and spiritual context. Although it established a tradition of interpretations and symbolizations that were employed in future apocalyptic expressions of crisis, each of those expressions must be viewed as a singular event in a singular historical situation. On the other hand, if one looks upon apocalypse as an existential phenomenon, as a particular reaction to experiences of suffering, there seems to be something anthropologically constant. This is not a distinguishing trait of the apocalypse itself, however, but rather of the human precondition of an otherwise historically contingent phenomenon.

In *Anamnesis*, Eric Veoeglin has interpreted the myth of the birth of Eros, as told in Plato's *Symposium*, as a symbolic description of the "in-between" character of human existence, that is, between ignorance and

16 E. Voegelin, *The Ecumenic Age*, op. cit., p. 26.

wisdom, mortality and immortality, temporal and eternal being.[17] The polies of the existential tension, whose content can be accentuated in several ways, receive a specific accent in this particular myth: Eros is the son of Poros (fullness, plenitude) and Penia (want, deficiency). Thus the myth calls attention to a particular dimension of the *conditio humana*: that we all have experiences of different levels of deficiency as well as of plenitude, experiences that are not stable, but change incessantly. These changes are experienced by us as a tension. More precisely, what is experienced are movements within a field of tension between the poles of deficiency and plenitude. The experience is never of deficiency or plenitude as exclusive entities. Even if we come very close to one of the poles, the tension to the other is maintained as a painful or hopeful possibility. The daimon Eros, who represents the tension, points to the fact that our movements in the field of tension between deficiency and plenitude are not aimless; the tension is directed toward the pole of plenitude. Human beings strive for the possibility of achieving plenitude, or happiness, as a perfect and permanent condition, though in actuality, humanity never escapes the experience of deficiency.

Plato's myth is meant to tell human beings that if they make room in their souls for the daimon Eros, that is, if they actualize their love for wisdom and immortality, they will move toward the pole of immortality and plenitude. However, the tension between deficiency and plenitude may be experienced not only as a loving movement toward plenitude. It also can produce fear, hate, and indignation if the destructive forces of want and imperfection are experienced as overwhelming. Ernst Bloch, one of the most ardent apocalyptic visionaries of twentieth-century Germany, has expressed this possibility: "However, where to go with these feelings of oneself, with this indelible being of that given Ego? For most human beings it is not pleasant to be born with this malicious heart, with these fixed grades of talent, whereby for those bearing self-hatred, the envy of others who seem to be favored without reason becomes even more a poison instead of a palliative. And does all that not lead further to the real enigma, to the revolt against the constellation as such, which causes us to be born into this particular social position, these particular chances, this particular time?"[18]

---

17   E. Voegelin, *Anamnesis*, pp. 266–269.
18   This is my translation of Ernst Bloch, *Geist der Utopie*, Berlin, 1923, p. 340.

Thus, the tension between deficiency and plenitude can be experienced and interpreted in very different ways. I understand the apocalypse as the symbolization of a specific exegesis of such experiences. The exegeses of the experiences of tension called "apocalyptic" obviously mark the tearing point of that tension. The overstretching of the tension up to the point of rupture is expressed by the tendency to break the tension between deficiency and plenitude into hypostatized entities that form a moral as well as temporal dualism. This particular type of interpreting experiences of tension, along with its particular symbols, distinguished the apocalyptic from other modes of interpreting such experiences, for instance the Platonic one.

In *Die politischen Religionen*, Eric Voegelin analyzed the motivating experiences of a young National Socialist poet, Gerhard Schumann, whose experiences led to a rupture of the existential tension.[19] Voegelin was the first, to my knowledge, to take into account National Socialist literature for such an analysis. He also noted in passing the apocalyptic overtones of Schumann's exegesis. With respect to the apocalyptic expression of an existential crisis, one can carry Voegelin's analysis even further. I am quoting, in prose translation, a sonnet, which Voegelin drew upon, too.

Then the night came. The One stood up and labored hard.
And blood flew from his eyes whose view
Faded away from the terrible horrors
That pressed from the vale up to the peak.

A cry of distress went up and broke shrill and full of fear.
Despair groped with a last grasp into the void.
He, in revolt, and trembling under the heavy burden,
Until the command forced him unto his knees.

But when he rose the glow of fire
Of the chosen dazzled around his head. And descending
He carried the torch into the night.

19 E. Voegelin, *Die politischen Religionen*, Schriftenreihe "Ausblicke," Vienna, 1938, pp. 57–61.

The millions bent down to him in silence.
Redeemed. The heaven flared with the glow of morning.
The sun went up. And with it grew the Reich.[20]

The poem not only expresses the political and social, but also the existential longing for salvation. Hitler's political struggle is modeled after the agony of Jesus in the garden of Gethsemane. The longing for and the promise of salvation is expressed with the typical excitement and urgency of an apocalyptic vision. Also typical is the symbolic dualism of "darkness" and "light," which symbolizes not only the contrast between the old deficient existence and the new perfect one, but also the contrast between death and life. The association with Jesus' agony suggests that Hitler, like Jesus, has defeated death.

The experience of death is, among the experiences of human deficiency, the most extreme; it marks indeed the core of the existential apocalypse. It may be recalled that chapter 21, verse 4 of the Revelation of John culminates in the promise: "There shall be an end to death, and to mourning and crying and pain; for the old order has passed away!" Ernst Bloch, too, although belonging to a different ideological camp than Gerhard Schumann, discloses the revolt against death as the central motivating force for his apocalyptic visions. From his first book, *Geist der Utopie*, he again and again brings passionate and bitter accusations against the destiny of human existence: "It is horrible to live and work in such a way and afterwards we are thrown into the grave. For a short time it was light, a mysteriously promising beginning . . . and then life turns into nothing, beyond all endurance, as though even before there would have been nothing, as though, even if one added a thousand beginnings, in view of this nothing, in view of this shallow and, at the same time, unfathomably deep hollow, no personal history had existed at all. And it is something so unimaginably alien to become blind, cold, rotten, with eyes fallen in and deep down in a narrow, dark, airless, tightly zincified coffin."[21] Later, in his major work of the forties, *Das Prinzip Hoffnung*, he characterized death as "the power of the

---

20   This is my rendering of Gerhard Schumann, *Die Lieder vom Reich*, Munich, 1936, p. 20.
21   This is my translation of Ernst Bloch, *Geist der Utopie*, Leipzig, 1918, p. 419.

strongest Non-Utopia."[22] The desperation in view of the prospect to be finally defeated by this power caused his "revolt against the constellation as such"[23] and made him hope "to find an escape from death."[24]

Since the revolt against death can be found in numerous apocalyptic visions (I could have added many more examples), one can conclude that the existential tension between deficiency and plenitude, from which the revolt against death follows, is an anthropological precondition for apocalyptic reactions. This existential tension, however, does not explain the particular form of reactions called apocalyptic. It does not explain why somebody turns to an apocalyptic worldview at all, or why, and under what circumstances, a social field of consciousness of apocalyptic character is constituted.

It has been noted that apocalyptic visions are elicited by experiences of crisis, or, to be more precise, by experiences of political and social oppression, existential and spiritual threat, and by the almost more depressing experiences that life and history are meaningless. These experiences are interpreted as proof of an existing crisis. The precondition for interpreting this crisis as the utmost and final one, that is, as an extreme situation that cannot be resolved by "normal" measures, is a differentiated exegesis of experiences pertaining to the *conditio humana* and the meaning of history. The tension between deficiency and plenitude could not become intolerable before the pole of plenitude became luminous, as the result of differentiated exegeses of those experiences of tension, as a divine absolute that, however, at the same time withdrew from men into a "beyond" of the cosmos. And the questions of the meaning and aim of history could not be raised until history had been constituted as a process that gave the impression of having a "meaning" as the result of the transcendent plenitude making itself present in singular events that seemed to constitute a course directed toward an aim.

The differentiation of the experiences of tension between deficiency and plenitude opened new horizons in comparison with the compact exegeses of these experiences in the cosmological myths. It offered a new

22 This is my translation of Ernst Bloch, *Das Prinzip Hoffnung*, vol. 3, Frankfurt, 1967, p. 1297.
23 This is my rendering of Bloch, *Geist der Utopie* (1918), p. 340.
24 Ibid., p. 331. This is my translation of the original: "das Kraut gegen den Tod zu finden."

promise that had never been known before, but it also increased the tension and made greater demands to endure it. In Israel the people as a whole were seen as the "subject" of this tension, as the people chosen by God; the tension between the transcendent truth and the inner-worldly existence was interpreted spiritually as well as politically and historically. Consequently, the tension became ever more intolerable the deeper Israel fell politically. A solution was found in the apocalyptic visions of the end of this process in the Book of Daniel; the process of pneumatic differentiation opened the way for the differentiated deformation of the apocalypse.

With the appearance of Jesus, the tension between deficiency and plenitude was differentiated even further, again with ambivalent consequences. In his chapter on Paul, in *The Ecumenic Age*, Voegelin laid the groundwork for detecting the point where the existential tension cannot be endured any longer and may be abolished by an apocalyptic speculation.[25] Again, it has to do with the extreme point of human deficiency: death. The experience that the promise of transcendent plenitude had become manifest in Jesus and the consequences of this experience for the relationship between human beings and God were so overwhelming for Paul that he used the symbols "transformation," "new birth," and "new man" to express adequately the existential significance of his perception. However, the insight that with the appearance of Jesus fulfillment has already become present in this world was bound to conflict with the experience that the structure of inner-worldly reality had not changed. Thus the problem was to endure the deficient condition of human existence, especially death, even though one has the experience of having come closer to salvation. In his letter to the Romans, Paul writes: "Know ye not that so many of us as were baptized into Jesus Christ were baptized into his death? Therefore, we are buried with him by baptism into death: that like as Christ was raised up from the dead by the glory of the Father, even so we also should walk in newness of life. For if we have been planted together in the likeness of his death, we shall be also in the likeness of his resurrection: Knowing this that our old man is crucified with him, that the body of sin might be destroyed, that henceforth we should not serve sin."[26]

Again and again Paul tried in this way to establish the existential balance

25 E. Voegelin, *The Ecumenic Age*, op. cit., pp. 239–271.
26 Rom. 6:3–6.

between the lasting experiences of deficiency and the consciousness of already being redeemed through Jesus and changed into a "new man." But this was not easy. The conviction that transcendent plenitude has become present in this world through Jesus caused euphoria, but also the impatient yearning to see redemption completed. At the same time the fear remained of falling back into the "darkness" of deficiency, as Paul indicated in his first letter to the Thessalonians. Here, euphoria, impatience, and fear induced him to dissolve the existential tension and to express the apocalyptic expectation that those who were alive now would not have to taste death anymore, but would experience the liberation from all deficiency: "For this we say unto you by the word of the Lord, that we which are alive and remain unto the coming of the Lord shall not prevent them which are asleep. For the Lord himself shall descend from heaven with a shout, with the voice of the archangel, and with the trumpet of God: and the dead in Christ shall rise first. Then we which are alive and remain shall be caught up together with them in the clouds, to meet the Lord in the air: and so shall we ever be with the Lord."[27]

Paul demonstrated the ambivalent character of the differentiated experience of tension between deficiency and plenitude: the change of consciousness that opens new insights into the structure of this tension and of reality as a whole, that draws closer to the transcendent pole of plenitude and therefore is experienced as a transformation into a "new man," has to be balanced with the experience that the deficient condition of the world continues to exist. The "new man" who feels transformed due to the change of his consciousness may change his life accordingly, but remains bound to the existential conditions of the "old man." By contrast, the apocalyptic "new man" is the conception of a transformed human being projected into the future in order to free him from the bonds of deficiency. The more painful these bonds are experienced and, in addition, the greater the perils and afflictions from outside, the more such a solution may suggest itself. The apocalyptic vision of John of Patmos was motivated by two factors: growing impatience, because the Parousia did not come; and suffering from the deficient reality that seemed to have reached a point past endurance, because Christians suffered severely from injustice, persecution, and oppression under the reign of Domitian.

27   I Thess. 4:15–17.

The examples mentioned so far—few but paradigmatic—can explain, with regard to motivating experiences, the existential meaning of apocalyptic visions as well as the fact that they imply, or even formulate, a speculation on history and its meaning. Motivating experiences can also make plausible why someone becomes an apocalyptic visionary. These experiences, however, do not offer sufficient reasons why a particular individual makes the existential decision for or against the apocalyptic turn; this remains a mystery.

If apocalyptic exegeses of experiences constitute a social field of consciousness, particular conditions and incidents of a social character are necessary, or— in variation of Voegelin's definition—a social field in which the exegeses of apocalyptic visionaries are understood by other people "who accept them as their own and make them into the motive of their habitual actions."[28] The precondition for such an acceptance is a situation that can be understood as a crisis (as characterized before) and the inability to maintain existential balance in distressing situations, or, what is virtually the same thing, the habitual tendency to resort to apocalyptic interpretations in situations of crisis. In twentieth-century Germany a social field of apocalyptic consciousness with all the characteristics mentioned above has been conspicuous.[29]

Apocalyptic interpretations of particular situations must be expressed verbally or visually, so that they can be understood by others. The whole set of verbal or visual elements—the structure of tales or dramatic scenes, personages, and images of literary or figurative representations, etc.—can be viewed as the "symbolization" of the pertinent exegesis. It is one of Voegelin's major achievements, in my opinion, that he contributed considerably to the clarification of fundamental problems of hermeneutics, with his notions of "experience," "exegesis of experience," and "symbolization," as well as "equivalences of experiences and symbolization."

If we analyze symbols as the exegetic means to interpret experiences, we refer to experiences as though they were given "things." However, experiences are not "given" with the symbols, even if they are represented very concretely and in detail. There always remains a difference between the invisible

28 E. Voegelin, *Anamnesis*, op. cit., p. 342.
29 In the present context I can only state this as a stand-alone fact. For detailed evidence see my earlier work, *The Apocalypse in Germany*, op. cit.

experiences, which are not "things," and the material significance of the symbols. If we make experiences the subject matter of our analysis, e.g., experiences of tension between deficiency and plenitude, the linguistic instruments of our analysis—the words "deficiency," "plenitude," and "tension"—are again symbols that only seem to enable us to lay hands on the subject matter. Also, this difference can be seen as a tension that cannot be dissolved, but we can understand and interpret it by moving within this tension. Plato used the myth of the birth of Eros for talking about the in-between existence of human beings, because myth does not know a contrast between "image" and "object"; in Ernst Cassirer's words: "the 'image' does not represent an 'object—it is the object."[30] Plato established the distance that has to be observed if one talks about experiences by putting the myth of the birth of Eros into the mouth of the prophetess Diotima. Her tale is reported by Socrates at the Symposium; and several years later Aristodemos, who was present then, retells the story to one Apollodoros who, again several years later, gives the report to his friends. Plato thus treats the "object" as the report of a report of the tale of a myth in order to relativize as far as possible the "object-character" of the myth. If we cannot use the same means, we must at least be conscious of that difference when we talk about experiences and symbols.

The problem of how to talk about experiences and how to analyze symbols adequately is aggravated by the fact that symbols may constitute traditions in which the original exegetic connection between motivating experiences and symbolization has been lost. This problem is of particular import if one deals with the apocalypse, because there is a specific and long-lasting symbolic tradition. I will assign some last considerations to this problem.

The symbolic appearance of apocalyptic visions cannot be separated from their content. The apocalyptic riders, the whore Babylon, the destruction of the sinful world, the New Jerusalem, were taken up in works of literature and the visual arts not only as subjects of formal interest, even if they often appear like mere quotations. The images of the apocalyptic tradition were taken up because they expressed something that recipients saw, felt, feared, or hoped in the same or in a similar way. Because of this, those

30 Ernst Cassirer, *Philosophie der symbolischen Formen*, vol. 2, 6th ed., Darmstadt, 1973, p. 51.

images were, in most cases, not only "quoted." Writers and artists, philosophers, theologians, and politicians found that those images could lend themselves to representing their feelings, experiences, and intentions. However, since these were their own feelings and intentions and not those of John of Patmos, they tried at the same time to express their singular character. They added new meaning to the traditional images, and accordingly new forms of articulation were created. The new forms were the result of new exegeses of experiences, but if one considers that the new forms modified traditional ones, one must conclude that the motivating experiences and intentions were equivalent. The same conclusion must be drawn if we consider verbal or visual images and other formal elements that cannot be traced back to traditional precedents, but nonetheless give the impression of being "apocalyptic." This impression can emerge only because there are similarities—if not between particular images, then perhaps similarities of form, structure, or semantics. Obviously, the commonness or similarity of symbolizations may be the original result of exegeses of experiences that are equivalences of those of the apocalyptic tradition.

The aesthetic characteristics that express the commonness of apocalyptic texts are therefore not only the result of a particular tradition but are generated, within this tradition or originally, by equivalent exegeses of experiences. The understanding of the equivalences of experiences and symbolization, and the understanding that the structure of symbolic forms represents the experiential structure of the soul, enable the differentiated analysis of a particular apocalyptic symbolization. Thus the apocalyptic visions of the twentieth century can be understood and analyzed, on the one hand, as historically singular phenomena, motivated by experiences that are rooted in their historical context; and, on the other hand, they can be rightly called "apocalyptic," which means that they can be ascribed to a tradition constituted by the Book of Daniel and the Revelation of John. The analysis of the equivalences of experiences and symbolization makes it possible to carry the investigation as the analysis of an existential syndrome as well as, considering the equivalences of equivalences, of an epochal phenomenon.

Rereading Eric Voegelin's *Order and History*[1]

The republication of *Order and History* in the *Collected Works* edition offers an apposite opportunity to reread Eric Voegelin's *magnum opus*, and invites a reappraisal, for almost fifty years have passed since the original publication of the first three volumes (1956/57) and almost twenty since Voegelin's death (1985). Before I set out to present the results of my renewed reading of *Order and History*, a few personal remarks are in order. Being neither a philosopher nor a political scientist, my perspective on Voegelin's work has been characterized by disciplinary distance but, at the same time, by scholarly as well as personal proximity. As a student of Voegelin's at the University of Munich in the 1960s, I "grew up" with the first three volumes of *Order and History* and Voegelin's other works. Although Political Science was not my "major," Voegelin's theoretical approach as well as the interdisciplinary scope of his scholarship was the strongest and most attractive stimulus of my student years and had lasting effect on my subsequent scholarly endeavors. During my postdoctoral research at Stanford University in 1972 and 1973, I witnessed the final stages of Voegelin's writing and completing of volume IV of *Order and History*, *The Ecumenic Age*, published in 1974. During subsequent visits, Voegelin entrusted to me—a frequent practice of his toward former students and friends in order to draw them into discussions—typescripts of newly written essays that were meant to become part of volume V, *In Search of Order*, like the chapter *The Beginning of the Beginning*, or that formed part of the context of this final volume, like *The Beginning and the Beyond*, also published posthumously.[2]

---

1   First published in *International Journal of the Classical Tradition* (IJCT) 11.1 (Summer 2004), pp. 80–94.

2   *The Collected Works of Eric Voegelin*, vol. 28: *What Is History? And Other Late Unpublished Writings*, edited with an Introduction by Thomas A. Hollweck and Paul Caringella, Baton Rouge and London, 1990.

For a reviewer of *Order and History* who has been familiar with Voegelin's work for more than forty years, yet is not an expert in all of the pertinent fields, it is advisable to control rereading impressions by consulting the secondary studies on Voegelin that have been published in recent years as well as older reviews, and especially the introductions written for the republication of *Order and History* in the *Collected Works* edition. Furthermore, a German translation of *Order and History* is in the process of being published, and the volumes of this edition also contain very knowledgeable introductions and epilogues.[3]

A survey of Voegelin's *magnum opus* requires various perspectives, considering the time span that lies between the first three volumes of 1956/57 and the fifth volume, published posthumously in 1987, and considering the developments or even 'breaks' in Voegelin's thinking during the last twenty years of his life, as reflected in *The Ecumenic Age* and *In Search of Order*. A first perspective must examine the individual volumes and look for the lasting significance of the respective material studies, especially with regard to the first three volumes that were published almost fifty years ago. Secondly, the developments and 'breaks' in the ongoing series mentioned above have to be evaluated. Finally, a comprehensive appraisal of *Order and History* as a whole is certainly desirable, if at all possible. The publishing history and the changing structure of *Order and History* both suggest that these three perspectives cannot always be neatly kept separate in the course of this review.

The first three volumes of *Order and History* themselves represented a break with a preceding monumental work of Voegelin's, the *History of Political Ideas*, almost complete in the early fifties but never published during Voegelin's lifetime.[4] Voegelin used the first parts of the *History of Political Ideas* as a material basis for the first three volumes of *Order and History*,

---

3   Eric Voegelin, *Ordnung und Geschichte*, Peter J. Opitz and Dietmar Herz, eds., Munich 2002 seq. The original five volumes have been divided, for the purpose of this edition, into ten volumes; so far vols. I and IV–VII have been published.

4   With the exception of one portion, see Eric Voegelin, *From Enlightenment to Revolution*, John H. Hallowell, ed., Durham, N.C., 1975. Meanwhile, the *History of Political Ideas* has been published as part of *The Collected Works of Eric Voegelin*, vols. 19–26, Columbia and London, 1997–1999.

but revised and expanded the previous text and, above all, refashioned it in accordance with his new theoretical concept, developed in 1951 while he was preparing the Walgreen Lectures at the University of Chicago, published under the title *The New Science of Politics*.[5] Voegelin himself explained succinctly why he abandoned the *History of Political Ideas* and set out afresh in his *Autobiographical Reflections*: "I had to give up 'ideas' as objects of a history and establish the experience of reality—personal, social, historical, cosmic—as the reality to be explored historically. These experiences, however, one could explore only by exploring their articulation through symbols."[6] In retrospect, these sentences captured the most important principle of Voegelin's new approach, as outlined in the Preface and Introduction to *Israel and Revelation*: To understand "the order of man, society, and history to the extent to which it has become accessible to science," one cannot resort to "ideas" as "objects" of study, but must take recourse to man's experience as a participant in the "primordial community of being"—God and man, world and society—and must analyze man's endeavors to endow his experiences with meaning in symbolic forms that constitute "truth concerning the order of being of which the order of society is a part."[7]

Order and History was meant, as Voegelin summarized at the end of the Preface to vol. I, to be "a philosophical inquiry concerning the order of human existence in society and history."[8] This was a concept commonly labelled "philosophy of history," and that Voegelin did indeed aspire to this philosophical genre is demonstrated by his references to, and discussions with, Toynbee, Jaspers, and Spengler in the first three volumes, especially in volumes I and II. At the same time, however, he claimed, in comparison with those philosophers

---

5   The history of the *History of Political Ideas*, the development and final abandonment of this work in favor of *Order and History*, has been very well documented by Thomas A. Hollweck, Ellis Sandoz, and Athanasios Moulakis in their introductions to *The Collected Works of Eric Voegelin*, vol. 19; *History of Political Ideas*, vol. I; *Hellenism, Rome, and Early Christianity*, edited with an Introduction by Athanasiois Moulakis, Columbia and London, 1997, pp. 1–57.

6   E. Voegelin, *Autobiographical Reflections*, edited with an Introduction by Ellis Sandoz, Baton Rouge and London, 1989, p. 80.

7   *Israel and Revelation*, op. cit., pp. 24, 39.

8   Ibid., p. 24.

of history, to offer a new approach to philosophizing about the history of mankind and, consequently, offer new insights. And Voegelin still remained a political scientist. The broad philosophical perspective notwithstanding, his "philosophical inquiry" clearly had political and social relevance, always including analyses of political and social order and disorder. Above all, these analyses, as well as the whole enterprise, were motivated by the ideological and political disorder of his time. The "search for truth concerning the order of being" emanates, as Voegelin pointed out, "from a man's awareness of his existence in untruth." Thus, the enterprise of *Order and History* was also meant to have a "remedial effect" for contemporary society.[9]

The first sentence of *Order and History* reads: "The order of history emerges from the history of order." Consequently, the program of *Order and History*, as envisaged in vol. I, is to lay out and analyze "a sequence of orders, intelligibly connected with one another as advances toward, or recessions from, an adequate symbolization of truth concerning the order of being of which the order of society is a part."[10] The first three volumes, covering the civilizations of the ancient Near East, Mesopotamia and Egypt, Israel, archaic Greece and the Hellenic Polis, and finally Plato and Aristotle, deals with three major forms of symbolizations: the compact myth of ancient cosmological societies and the differentiated symbolisms of revelation and philosophy in Israel and Hellas. The breaks with the "compactness" of the cosmological myth that occurred independently of each other Voegelin called "leaps in being";[11] they produced, in Voegelin's view, "a new truth about the order of being":[12] revelation with consequences primarily for the order of history and the order of society in its immediacy under God, philosophy with consequences for the order of the psyche of man, directed toward the *agathon*. Although Voegelin already cautioned the reader on the first page of *Order and History* that "there is no simple pattern of progress or cycles running through history"[13] (a foreshadowing of the later revision

9   Ibid.
10   Ibid., p. 19.
11   See especially, *Israel and Revelation*, op. cit., pp. 48, 52, 89–90; *The World of the Polis*, pp. 67–90.
12   *The World of the Polis*, op. cit., p. 67.
13   *Israel and Revelation*, op. cit., p. 19.

of his concept), the first three volumes give the impression of a "sequence," of a process of differentiation that culminates—the equivalence of revelation and philosophy notwithstanding—in Plato.

The general principles of Voegelin's study, the supposition of man's participatory existence within the "quarternarian structure" of God and man, world and society;[14] the consideration of symbolic forms as expressions or "exegeses" of experiences; the understanding that symbols are self-interpretations of experiences within the "quarternarian" field of existence with the goal to endow these experiences with meaning and finally to arrive at "truth concerning the order of being"; the insight that there are stages of compactness and differentiation of experiences and symbolization as well as recessions and degradations, and, in addition, the methodological principle that "theory" is not an *a priori* dogma, but the result of carefully conducted material studies—these principles were truly innovative and yielded new, and often surprising, insights. Thus, Voegelin's overall view and many of his results have lost nothing of their merit (depending, of course, on whether one goes along with his philosophical and methodological approach). If one goes into detail, however, the situation looks slightly different.

It is no surprise that after almost half a century we detect shortcomings and doubtful, even erroneous, interpretations in the first three volumes of *Order and History*. This is due to the fact that scholarship has advanced, that a wealth of new material has been made accessible during that period of time, especially with respect to the societies of Mesopotamia, Egypt, Israel, the Minoan and Mycenaean cultures. There are new and better translations of texts, more precise datings, new archeological findings, more sophisticated analyses in the pertinent disciplines of orientalism, Egyptology, biblical theology, archeology, philology of old oriental languages. Voegelin himself was always aware that research would continue and that his analyses did not have the character of "last words." A second reason for certain shortcomings can be seen in Voegelin's selection of material for the basis of his study. And finally, we look back now to the first three volumes of *Order and History* with an awareness of the developments and advances Voegelin himself made in his later work.

14 Ibid., p. 39.

That Voegelin began his study with the ancient civilizations of Mesopotamia and Egypt was quite unusual for the time, the works of Spengler and Toynbee notwithstanding. Not an orientalist himself, he had to resort to pertinent scholarly investigations and to translations of texts. Yet, it was his good fortune that especially the works of the Chicago school of orientalists, above all Henri Frankfort's and John A. Wilson's, provided a highly advanced "state of the science.." Not equally reliable were the translations Voegelin had to use, nor their datings. The 'Memphite Theology', for instance, is apparently more than 2000 years younger than Voegelin had to assume and therefore cannot maintain the significance Voegelin ascribed to it.[15]

Contemporary orientalists and Egyptologists list as shortcomings of Voegelin's interpretations of the Mesopotamian and Egyptian civilizations his selection of texts, excluding important ones that would have allowed a more complex image of these civilizations; they criticize a certain negligence of pragmatic aspects, especially the importance of rites for the order and self-interpretation of the pertinent societies, and they criticize some of Voegelin's interpretations as outdated. It is interesting, though, that especially renowned scholars, like the orientalist Peter Machinist and the Egyptologist Jan Assmann, despite their criticism still appreciate Voegelin's general approach as well as some of his particular analyses, as for instance the interpretation of "divine manifestation in the Pharaoh."[16] They both maintain that the history of the Mesopotamian societies and of Egypt was more complicated than Voegelin's presentation suggested and, above all, that these civilizations were not as mythologically 'compact' as Voegelin's image of the cosmological societies implied—a problem that Voegelin himself tried to solve later on with his concept of "historiogenesis." But they nonetheless value this "first attempt to do justice to the forms of thinking of the early civilizations in a comprehensive theory of evolution," and they appreciate Voegelin as a "pioneer and stimulating mind" who challenges continuous research and thinking, refutation, contradiction, as well as approval."[17]

15 Ibid., pp. 127–135.
16 Ibid., pp. 106–121.
17 See the introduction and epilogues by Jan Assmann and Peter Machinist in,

We encounter a similar mixture of criticism and appreciation with respect to Voegelin's analysis of Israel. In an early review, H. H. Rowley had criticized that Voegelin accentuated "paradigmatic history" while neglecting "pragmatic history," and he warned that "it is important to establish how far the history is reliable in a work which is devoted to *Order and History*."[18] This criticism is still maintained in recent biblical theology and Jewish thought, as for instance by Bernhard W. Anderson and Moshe Idel, as well as by Maurice P. Hogan in his introduction to *Israel and Revelation*. And in a way similar to Machinists's and Assmann's critique, Moshe Idel criticizes Voegelin's "marginalization of ritual." In his view, ritual, in interrelationship with myth, played a much more important role in the "general economy of Judaism" than Voegelin recognized.[19] In addition, recent archeological, historical, and philological research suggests that the history of pre-exile Judaism is even more characterized by "pluralistic symbolization" than Voegelin admitted and that, in Anderson's view, this "is also evident in the Bible."[20]

Although biblical studies have moved in new directions during recent decades, as Hogan states in his introduction to vol. I, biblical hermeneutics, for all its new methods and approaches, "still needs a philosophy of history such as Voegelin presents."[21] Thus Voegelin's study is still important because of its philosophical perspective on what makes Israel exceptional: that in Israel a breakthrough to a more differentiated understanding of "the order of being of which the order of society is a part" occurred, cast in the symbolization of the Exodus from the cosmological society of Egypt and the

Eric Voegelin, *Ordnung und Geschichte*, vol. I: *Die kosmologischen Reiche des Alten Orients, Mesopotamien und Ägypten*, Jan Assmann, ed., Munich 2002; quotations from pp. 17, 224 (my translation).

18　H. H. Rowley, "Review of *Israel and Revelation*, *Journal of Biblical Literature*," 1958, p. 157.

19　Bernhard W. Anderson, "Revisiting Voegelin's *Israel and Revelation* after Twenty-Five Years"; Moshe Idel, "Voegelin's *Israel and Revelation*: Some Observations"; both in Glenn Hughes, Steven A. McKnight, Geoffrey L. Price, eds., *Politics, Order and History. Essays on the Work of Eric Voegelin*, Sheffield, 2001, pp. 284–326; see especially, pp. 290, 309–310.

20　Ibid., p. 295.

21　*Israel and Revelation*, op. cit., p. 13.

revelation of the transcendent God in the thornbush episode, and that, in consequence, Israel developed an understanding of being a people with a "history" in the presence of the transcendent God and thus created history as a symbolic form of existence.

It was Voegelin's problem, and it remains one for many retrospective evaluations, that he was an "outsider" for orientalists, classicists, theologians, philosophers, and historians who could point to shortcomings from their respective professional viewpoints. Not very often do we find specialists who are able to combine their (justified) criticism of Voegelin's handling of certain subject matters or particular details with a congenial understanding of the theoretical approach and general importance of his enterprise. Such a balanced evaluation is, however, presented by Athanasios Moulakis in his competent and highly informative introduction to vol. II of *Order and History, The World of the Polis*. Again, as in Voegelin's treatment of the older civilizations in vol. I, some of his interpretations, especially with respect to the Minoan and Mycenaean cultures, have been proven erroneous or at least problematic by more recent archeological and historical studies. And again, Voegelin is not so much interested in the pragmatic history of the Greek *poleis*, the internal constitutional processes and the process of colonization. His focal point is the process of spiritual symbolization. There is another reason for Voegelin's neglecting several aspects of Greek history and for some of his questionable interpretations, as Moulakis has pointed out: The structure of vol. II, as well as the selection and interpretation of materials, is governed by the direction to Plato as the final breakthrough of philosophy, the second "leap in being." The intention to construct a continuity that leads to the telos of Platonic philosophy determines and, as Moulakis remarks, "in many respects overdetermines" Voegelin's interpretations (e.g. of the Minoan culture, of Homer and Solon), and his idealized image of the Athens of Marathon in contrast to Plato's Athens.[22] On the other hand, Voegelin clearly worked out that in Hellas the break with the myth and the differentiation between transcendence and immanence was a gradual process and that therefore the cosmology of the early Greek societies was different from that of the ancient oriental ones. He recognized that Homer's epic already was no longer "cosmological," and, of course, he attributed decisive

22   *The World of the Polis*, op. cit., p. 27.

steps in the development toward the final breakthrough of philosophy to the Pre-Socratics, in particular to Parmenides, and even to the Sophists, despite his general criticism of their method.

In his introduction to vol. II, Moulakis deplores, in parallel to some critiques of vol. I, Voegel's neglect of non-verbal forms of symbolization that would have provided additional insights: rituals and games and, above all, the visual arts: architecture, sculpture, vase painting.[23] This criticism reflects recent developments in the disciplines of cultural history or cultural studies (*Kulturwissenschaft*) with an increased interest in the symbolic meaning of "material" culture. Non-verbal symbolizations were not ignored by Voegelin. I remember that in the early 1970s Voegelin visited prehistoric, in particular megalithic, monuments and archeological sites in Turkey, Malta, England, and Ireland, and at the same time engaged in intensive discussions and correspondence with the prehistorian and ethnologist Marie E. P. König, who had published, among other pertinent studies, a book on the symbolic meaning of prehistoric pictographs.[24] Voegelin showed so much interest in this matter that speculations arose on whether he might write a volume 'zero' for *Order and History* on prehistoric orders of symbolization. Obviously, he did not. Certainly, the main reason was that in analyzing prehistoric non-verbal symbols one does not stand on very firm ground. This episode seems to be symptomatic for Voegelin's general tendency to maintain a distance from interpretations of non-verbal symbolic forms. In his view, only language can express symbols of order in their relationship to engendering of experiences on the differentiated level he was interested in; thus he had to concentrate on written sources.

In vol. III, *Plato and Aristotle*, Voegelin engaged in his most detailed and penetrating interpretation of single authors' works, especially of Plato's dialogues. Nonetheless, "pragmatic" history still plays a role, if only—although this is of great importance—as the "background" of motivating experiences. The corruption and degradation of the *polis* presented, in Voegelin's view, a decisive stimulus for Plato to concentrate his philosophy on the soul of the individual as the center of experiencing the order of

---

23 Ibid., pp. 38, 46.
24 Marie E. P. König, *Am Anfang der Kultur. Die Zeichensprache des frühen Menschen*, Berlin, 1973.

being. In the *Republic*, Voegelin argued, Plato "issued the appeal of the Idea, and was still bound to the polis through his hope for a response." Still, for Voegelin the *Republic* was neither a "utopian" vision nor a call for action, but an existential and political paradigm. From the *Phaedrus* on, however, Plato was "resigned to the fact that the polis has rejected his appeal," the *Phaedrus* is "the manifesto that announces the emigration of the spirit from the polis."[25] As Voegelin saw it, the turn away from deliberating on the political order of the polis culminated in the *Laws,* where, instead, the order of the individual soul becomes the center of contemplation.

Thus, Plato's work for Voegelin had not only meaning for the "history of order," but also existential meaning. There was a greater distance between Plato's (and Aristotle's) works and the order of the surrounding society than there had been in the cosmological societies and even in Israel between the creators of symbolic order and the pragmatic order of society. Whereas the revelatory "leap in being" in Israel constituted the historical existence of the chosen people in the present under God, the breakthrough of the parallel differentiation of philosophy brought to consciousness the divine order of being that might also extend into society and history, but has its center in the soul of the philosopher. The lasting existential meaning of— especially—Plato's philosophy is clearly shown by Voegelin's placing himself in a "Platonic position" with respect to the ideological and political corruption of his own time.[26]

For both volumes II and III, Voegelin took advantage of the pioneering studies of Bruno Snell, Werner Jäger, and Francis M. Cornford, and departed from their views in essential points, as was his custom even when he was influenced by, and in general accordance with, brilliant scholarship. In comparison with Aristotle, Plato clearly had pivotal importance for Voegelin, as shown not only by the respective internal proportions of vol. III, but also by the recurrent treatment of Plato in volumes IV and V. Voegelin's presentation of Aristotle was more in accord with the academic scholarship of his time than his understanding of Plato. He was indebted to a high degree to Werner Jäger's book on Aristotle (which is now considered to be outdated in many respects).[27] For Voegelin, Aristotle was the "theoretician," while

25   E. Voegelin, *Plato and Aristotle*, op. cit., p. 193.
26   Ibid., p. 91.
27   Cf. ibid., p. 325, note 1, with additional references.

Plato seemed closer to the motivating experiences of symbols. It was mainly Voegelin's persistent search for the interrelationship between experiences and symbolization, I think, that earned him raised eyebrows, to say the least, from certain Plato scholars, apart from his "occasionally shooting from the hip," as Dante Germino nicely put it in his introduction to *Plato and Aristotle*.[28] The "noetic" dimension of experiences, as Voegelin called it, was not to be separated from the motivating experiences in the field of politics and society; this was demonstrated in particular in the central chapter on the *Republic* with Voegelin's interpretation of the "way up" and the "way down" as symbols with existential as well as political meaning.[29] Again, we have to remember that Voegelin was after all a political scientist; Carl J. Friedrich put the accent correctly when in his review of 1958 he judged that Voegelin's "discourse is *political theory* in the highest sense."[30]

The relationship between Voegelin and scholarship on Plato was characterized mainly by mutual disregard, although in some cases there would have been points of convergence and the possibility of mutual benefit. An interesting and telling example is the philosophical debate about Plato's "unwritten doctrines." Of the older studies on this subject by Harold Cherniss, Cornelia J. de Vogel, Walter Bröcker, and others, Voegelin mentions only Cherniss with a reference in a footnote.[31] The books and articles by Konrad Gaiser and Hans-Joachim Krämer that dealt with the problem of Plato's "unwritten doctrines" on a new and highly sophisticated level, as well as subsequent studies, came out too late for *Plato and Aristotle*.[32] Apparently, Voegelin read Gaiser's

---

28 Ibid., p. 30.
29 Ibid., pp. 100–188.
30 Carl J. Friedrich, "Symbols of Order and History?" in *Jewish Frontier*, vol. XXV (1958), No. 12, p. 11 (emphasis my own).
31 E. Veogelin, *Plato and Aristotle*, p. 60, note 1.
32 Konrad Gaiser, *Platons ungeschriebene Lehre. Studien zur systematischen und geschichtlichen Begründung der Wissenschaften in der Platonischen Schule*, Stuttgart, 1963; ibid., ed., *Das Platonbild. Zehn Beiträge zum Platonverständnis*, Hildesheim, 1969; Hans-Joachim Krämer, *Arete bei Platon und Aristoteles. Zum Wesen und zur Geschichte der platonischen Ontologie*, Heidelberg, 1959; ibid., "Retraktationen zum Problem des esoterischen Platon," *Mus. Helvet.* 21 (1964), pp. 137–167; cf. also, Jürgen Wippern, ed., *Das Problem der ungeschriebenen Lehre Platons. Beiträge zum Verständnis der platonischen Prinzipien-*

book after finishing his own, but it seems that he did not make use of it for his later publications on Plato (nor is Voegelin mentioned in the studies referred to in note 31). Yet, there are important points of convergence: (1) Voegelin's constant stress on the symbolic quality of language as an exegetic expression of experiences and his perpetual warning against 'hypostasizing' symbols into "objects" of cognition, paralleling Plato's warning in the *Phaedrus* and in the *Second Letter* against trusting too much in the truth of a "written discourse" as opposed to the superior "living dialogue";[33] (2) the "mystic" quality attributed by Gaiser and others to the knowledge of the first principles in Plato's "unwritten doctrines"; which would seem to be in accordance with Voegelin's understanding of Plato as a "mystic philosopher";[34] (3) the center of this mystic quality, the accentuation of the "One" (*hen*) as an equivalence of the "Good" (*agathon*) of the written dialogues. In my opinion, the last point could have readily been integrated into Voegelin's interpretation of Plato. Probably, Voegelin stayed away from Plato's "unwritten doctrines" because he was skeptical about the trustworthiness of Aristotle's respective references to the *hen* in Plato's theory of ideas (not clearly substantiated by the dialogues),[35] not to mention the unreliability of the reports of Pythagoreanizing witnesses like Aristoxenos and later Platonists.

lehre, Darmstadt, 1972. The following studies, published after Voegelin's death, may be of service to readers interested in Plato's "unwritten doctrines": Thomas Alexander Szlezák, *Platon und die Schriftlichkeit der Philosophie. Interpretationen zu den frühen und mittleren Dialogen*, Berlin – New York, 1985; ibid., *Come leggere Platone*, Presentation by Giovanni Reale, ser. Problemi attuali, Milan, 1991; ibid., *Platon lessen*, Legenda 1, Stuttgart-Bad Cannstatt, 1993; Hans-Joachim Krämer, *Plato and the Foundations of Metaphysics: A Work on the Theories of the Principles and Unwritten Doctrines of Plato with a Collection of the Fundamental Documents*, edited and translated by John R. Catan, Albany, 1990; Giovanni Reale, *Per una nuova interpretazione di Platone*, Milan, 1997.

33 *Phaedrus*, 275–278; *Second Letter*, 314c, 341b–342, 344c–345c. Voegelin refers to these passages in *Plato and Aristotle*, op. cit., pp. 73–74.

34 For the 'mystic' aspect (and cognizant of the 'unwritten doctrines'), cf. Christoph Riedweg, *Mysterienterminologie bei Platon, Philon und Klemens von Alexandrien*, Untersuchungen zur antiken Literatur und Geschichte 26, Berlin – New York, 1987.

35 *Metaphysics*, 988a 10 f.; 988 b 4–5.

The first three volumes of *Order and History* formed a unit, based on the concept laid out in vol. I and reiterated in the fact of their swift publication all within one year. Seventeen years passed until the publication of vol. IV, under the title *The Ecumenic Age* instead of *Empire and Christianity*, as had been originally announced. The book came as a surprise for many Voegelin readers and even as a disappointment for some of them. Disappointed was, for instance, Carl J. Friedrich's expectation (in his review of vols. I-III) that in the following volumes "the Christian era is linked to these studies of Israel and Hellas as the final word on the meaning of man's existence, its order and its history."[36] Now, not only had Christianity disappeared from the title, but it also did not figure as the ultimate telos of a process of differentiation that ran from myth via revelation and philosophy to Christ. And Voegelin did not deal with the person of Jesus Christ, but with "The Pauline Vision of the Resurrected," contemplating on the "pneumatic" symbolization of experience as being equivalent to the "noetic" one—not from a Christian, but from a philosophical viewpoint.[37]

The perspective of *The Ecumenic Age* was much broader than originally projected. Taking the title seriously, the book included not only a chapter on the Chinese ecumene, but above all considerations on the consequences of ecumenic empires for historiographic thinking and general reflections on the process of history in the light of spiritual differentiations, as well as contemplations on universal humanity. Nonetheless, and this was the biggest surprise, there was no "final word," but a new beginning, as it seemed. The first sentence of the Introduction to vol. IV reads: "The present volume, *The Ecumenic Age*, breaks with the program I have developed for *Order and History* in the Preface to Volume I of the series."[38] In the Preface to vol. I, Voegelin had enumerated

36 Carl J. Friedrich, "Symbols of Order and History?" in *Jewish Frontier*, vol. XXV/12 (1958), p. 11.

37 Some of the critiques from a Christian viewpoint are presented in the Introduction to *The Ecumenic Age* (=*Order and History* IV), pp. 18–19, note 41. They include Frederick D. Wilhelmsen, "Professor Voegelin and the Christian Tradition," ibid., *Christianity and Political Philosophy*, Athens, Georgia, 1978, pp. 195–196, 201, 205; Bruce Douglass, "The Break in Voegelin's Program," in *Political Science Reviewer* 7 (1977), p. 14; Gerhart Niemeyer, "Eric Voegelin's Philosophy and the Drama of Mankind," in *Modern Age* 20 (1976), p. 34.

38 *The Ecumenic Age*, p. 45.

five types of order to be covered by his study: cosmological societies and the symbolic form of myth; the revelatory form of existence in history (Israel); the development of philosophy in Hellas; the multicivilizational empires since Alexander, and the emergence of Christianity; the modern national state, and the emergence of modern Gnosticism as the symbolic form of order. These five types of order and symbolization, Voegelin now explained, "turned out to be regrettably limited." He maintained that nothing was "wrong with the principle of the study" and that, with respect to the first three volumes, "there was really an advance in time from compact to differentiated experiences of reality and, correspondingly, an advance from compact to differentiated symbolizations of the order of being." But from a broader perspective that included the materials to be analyzed for the second sequence of volumes as well as a retrospective look at the preceding symbolizations of order, Voegelin realized that the empirical types of order could not be subordinated to an overall concept that insinuated a "course" of history. Thus, he conceded, the original, general conception "was untenable because it had not taken proper account of the important lines of meaning in history that did not run along lines of time."[39] The task could not be to construct the meaning *of* history, as so many philosophies of history had tried to do, but to trace and analyze the events where meaning *in* history had been experienced and symbolized.[40] In consequence, the analyses of *The Ecumenic Age* do not, as in the preceding volumes, follow a general chronological line, but move "through a web of meaning with a plurality of nodal points" and with several "dominant lines of meaning" reaching from cosmological civilizations up to modern times.[41] This complicated composition of the book does not make for easy reading.

A decisive stimulus for Voegelin's change of concept was the analytical clarification of a symbolism for which he coined the name "historiogenesis." He presented his analysis of this type of speculation in great detail in the first chapter of vol. IV.[42] By "historiogenesis," Voegelin meant a

---

39 Ibid., p. 46.
40 Cf. ibid., pp. 223–224, 251–252.
41 Ibid., p. 106.
42 First published in Eric Voegelin, *Anamnesis. Zur Theorie der Geschichte und Politik*, Munich, 1966, for *The Ecumenic Age*, revised and substantially expanded.

fourth type of cosmological symbolization, in addition to cosmogony, theogony, and anthropogony, a type of myth that constructed a "course" of history running from gods via heroes to dynasties and kings and that could be found in several cosmological societies. Proposing this type of speculation meant a certain revision of the "compactness" Voegelin had ascribed to the cosmological societies. On the other hand, the idea of a unilinear history apparently was not, as Voegelin previously had assumed, engendered by the differentiating events that led to the conception of history in Israel and later in Christianity, but turned out to be a cosmological symbolism. Consequently, he had to register the persistence of a "cosmological" type of speculation up to the modern philosophies of history of the eighteenth and nineteenth centuries (with different content, but the same structure) which raised the question: "What exactly was modern about modernity?"[43] This was a major reason for Voegelin himself not to fall in the trap of historiogenetic speculation in his own philosophy of history.

Apart from "historiogenesis," Voegelin introduced some other new terms in *The Ecumenic Age* in order to create precise linguistic instruments for central points of his analyses, as, for instance, "egophany" for the revolt of the "ego" against the divine order of being that became luminous in "theophanic" or "hierophanic" events. The most important term, however, which also became focal for Voegelin's subsequent philosophical contemplations, was the Greek *metaxy* (between). Voegelin derived it from Diotima's mythic tale about the birth of Eros and the discussion about love and the spiritual man (*daimonios aner*) in Plato's *Symposium*.[44] The word occurs there in the description of man's existence between ignorance and wisdom, between deficiency and plenitude, between mortality and immortality.[45] Now, "between" is just an ordinary preposition and one may question whether there is real textual evidence that Plato himself charged this particular word with philosophical meaning, however frequently it occurs. But it was a congenial stroke, I think, to capture with this simple preposition what indeed was contemplated in Plato's dialogue: the "in-between

43 *The Ecumenic Age*, pp. 51–52.
44 Already in *Anamnesis*, pp. 266–269; in *The Ecumenic Age*, pp. 245–246.
45 *Symposium*, 202–204.

existence" of man; and it is characteristic of Voegelin's interpretation of Plato that amounts to continued philosophizing "along Plato's line."[46]

The Ecumenic Age represented an additional "break," not so much with the first three volumes, but with the original program for the second sequence of volumes. In the Introduction to *The Ecumenic Age* Voegelin declared as his "conclusion" for revising the program: "The process of history, and such order as can be discerned in it, is not a story to be told from the beginning to its happy, or unhappy, end."[47] The original program of *Order and History* suggested a rather unhappy end: the Gnostic disorder of modernity. But the insight that the process of history is not a story to be told from the beginning to the end, but "a mystery in process of revelation," ruled out not only the tale of a consecutive sequence of differentiations but also the respective tale of the pertinent deformations.[48] Deformation of differentiations, Voegelin stated, "is a force in world history of the same magnitude as differentiation itself."[49] The obvious conclusion is that it does not run along lines of time any more than the process of differentiation.

For this but also for other reasons, the Gnosticism thesis that originally seemed to mark the final point of *Order and History* lost weight in *The Ecumenic Age* as well as in vol. V.[50] On several occasions before the publication

---

46 There are other Plato scholars who enter into interpretations in connection with the semantics of *metaxy* and *méson*: Giovanni Reale, *Eros dèmone mediatore e il gioco delle maschere nel Simposio di Platone*, Milan 1997 (cf. ibid., "Alles was tief ist, liebt die Maske," Thomas Alexander Szlezák, ed., *Platonisches Philosophieren. Zehn Vorträge zu Ehren Hans Joachim Krämers*, Spudasmata 82, Hildesheim – Zürich – New York, 2001, pp. 87–108. As for the "question whether there is real textual evidence that Plato himself charged this particular word (sc. *metaxy*) with philosophical meaning," see in the affirmative (even though the term is usually *méson* rather than *metaxy*) Konrad Gaiser, *Platons ungeschriebene Lehre*, chapters "Der mathematische und der werthafte Aspekt der 'Mitte': Platos Lehrvorträge 'Über das Gute,'" pp. 67–88, and "Die ontologische Mittelstellung der 'Mathematika' und die Seele," pp. 89–106.

47 *The Ecumenic Age*, p. 51.

48 Ibid.

49 Ibid., p. 86.

50 Some of Voegelin's critics, especially in Germany, still identify him solely with his Gnosticism thesis, due to the impact of *The New Science of Politics* (German translation: *Die neue Wissenschaft der Politik*, Munich, 1959) and *Wissenschaft,*

of *The Ecumenic Age,* Voegelin already had relativized his Gnosticism thesis, as, for instance, in his *Autobiographical Reflections,* dictated in 1973: "Since my first applications of Gnosticism to modern phenomena in *The New Science of Politics* and in 1959 in my study on *Science, Politics, and Gnosticism,*. I have had to revise my position." Although the "application of the category of Gnosticism to modern ideologies" was still valid in his view, he admitted that "in a more complete analysis, however, there are other factors to be considered in addition. One of these factors is the metastatic apocalypse deriving directly from the Israelite prophets."[51] In addition, he mentioned neo-Platonism and, on other occasions, hermeticism, alchemy, and magic.[52] In *The Ecumenic Age* the modified assessment of Gnosticism as only *one* component of modernity came into effect. On the one hand, it is true, Voegelin maintained his critical thrust against the "essential core" of Gnosticism, as he indicated in the Introduction: "The essential core is the enterprise of returning the pneuma in man from its state of alienation in the cosmos to the divine pneuma of the Beyond through action based on knowledge."[53] On the other hand, he now referred more explicitly to historical forms of Gnosticism as a "variable part of a Gnostic system," and he concluded for the treatment of Gnosticism in vol. IV: "The Gnostic deformation of consciousness must be put into the pragmatic and spiritual context of the Ecumenic Age."[54] This meant for antiquity that Voegelin placed

Politik und Gnosis, Munich, 1959 (English translation: *Science, Politics and Gnosticism,* Chicago 1968). The suspicion suggests that these critics have not read Voegelin's later work. See for instance, Richard Faber, "Eric Voegelin. Gnosis-Verdacht als polit(olog)isches Strategem," in Jacob Taubes, ed., *Gnosis und Politik* (= *Religionstheorie und politische Theologie,* ed. J. Taubes, vol. 3), München – Paderborn – Wien – Zürich 1987, pp. 230–248; Hubert Cancik, "Neuheiden und totaler Staat. Völkische Religion am Ende der Weimarer Republik" (1982), in *Antik-Modern. Beiträge zur römischen und deutsche Kulturgeschichte,* Richard Faber, ed., Stuttgart – Weimar, 1998, p. 202.

51 *Autobiographical Reflections,* p. 66. For a detailed discussion of Voegelin's Gnosticism thesis, cf. my article, "Gnosis, Apokalypse und Moderne," in *Politische Religion? Politik, Religion und Anthropologie im Werk Eric Voegelins,* Michael Ley, Heinrich Neisser, Gilbert Weiss, eds., Munich, 2003, pp. 63–75.

52 Ibid., pp. 63–64; *Autobiographical Reflections,* p. 67.

53 *The Ecumenic Age,* p. 66.

54 Ibid., p. 67.

the apocalypse, as it originated in Judaism, as an equivalent symbolism of revolt against the order of being alongside Gnostic speculations. If one interprets the Jewish apocalypse as a deviation from "prophetic pneumatism," as Voegelin did, one could even view the apocalypse as a predecessor in the process of pneumatic deformation.[55]

Voegelin now placed Gnosticism and apocalypse side by side as equivalent forces also when dealing with modern forms of political and spiritual disorder,[56] and it even seemed as though he wanted to introduce, with the combination of both, a new, modified general concept for the dominant characteristic of modernity, i.e., the revolt against the order of being through immanentization: "While these early (Gnostic) movements attempt to escape from the Metaxy by splitting its poles into the hypostases of this world and the Beyond, the *modern apocalyptic-Gnostic movements* attempt to abolish the Metaxy by transforming the Beyond into this world."[57]

In vol. V of *Order and History*, *In Search of Order*, Voegelin once again characterized what in his view was the "essential core" of Gnosticism and at the same time distinguished ancient from modern Gnosticism: "At the extreme of the revolt in consciousness, 'reality' and the 'Beyond' become two separate entities, two 'things', to be magically manipulated by suffering man for the purpose of either abolishing 'reality' altogether and escaping into the 'Beyond' or of forcing the order of the 'Beyond' into 'reality'. The first of the magic alternatives is preferred by the gnostics of antiquity, the second one by the modern gnostic thinkers."[58] The characteristic of the second variant is true rather of the *apocalyptic* movements of modernity, I think, if one understands "forcing" in a straightforward political and activist sense, and if one understands "the order of the 'Beyond'" that is to be obtained by force as the imagination of a state of redemption that produces, as we all know, inhuman perversion if realization is attempted. If, however, one understands "forcing" as a forcible speculation, one will indeed detect a relationship between Gnostic speculations of redemption and some modern thinkers, as,

55   Ibid., pp. 24–27.
56   Ibid., p. 96, cf. p. 243.
57   Ibid., p. 302, emphasis my own.
58   *In Search of Order*, p. 51.

for instance, Hegel, who for Voegelin was king's evidence for modern Gnosticism, or in the last century Ernst Bloch, who started out as an apocalypticist and later on confessed to "revolutionary Gnosis."[59]

Apart from the quotation cited above, there are only a few remarks concerning Gnosticism in vol. V. Instead of the title originally planned for the final volume of *Order and History*, *The Crisis of Western Civilization*, the volume now bore the title *In Search of Order*, thus shifting the accent from the negative to the positive, as it were, from the presentation and analysis of the disorder of the modern age to the existential quest for truth concerning the order of being.

In *Search of Order* was published posthumously as a fragment, it contained only two major essays, *The Beginning of the Beginning* and *Reflective Distance vs. Reflective Identity*. It seems that Voegelin had planned, at the time of completing *The Ecumenic Age* and in the following years, to use some other articles and essays for vol. V, published already during his lifetime or posthumously, like *The Gospel and Culture*, *Equivalences of Experience and Symbolization in History*, *On Hegel: A Study in Sorcery*, *The Moving Soul*, *The Beginning and the Beyond*.[60] But certainly he would have revised them for inclusion in vol. V, and since he did not complete that task and since, toward the end of his life, he apparently often referred to the two essays mentioned above as the core of volume V, the editor decided to include those two only. Nonetheless, the other essays, in particular the ones in the volume *Late Unpublished Writings*, must be seen as closely related to *In Search of Order*.

In *Search of Order* represented not a new 'break' with the preceding volume, but again a change with respect to theoretical approach and method. In terms of 'genre', it definitely was no longer an analytical story

---

59 Cf. my earlier work, *The Apocalypse in Germany*. Columbia and London, 2000, pp. 372–374.

60 Cf. Voegelin's notes in *The Ecumenic Age*, pp. 243, note 7, 251; note 9, 261; note 12, 264; note 14. These articles were subsequently published in *The Collected Works of Eric Voegelin*, vol. 12: *Published Essays 1966–1985*, edited with an Introduction by Ellis Sandoz, Baton Rouge and London, 1990; and in vol. 28: *What is History? And Other Late Unpublished Writings*, edited with an Introduction by Thomas A. Hollweck and Paul Caringella, Baton Rouge and London, 1990.

of the "history of order," but a philosophical meditation on the "order of history" concerning the topics Voegelin had been struggling with all the time: the beginning, and the end of history, the 'course' of history and meaning *in* history; the participatory existence of man and the tension of existential reality; the experience of untruth and the search for truth concerning the order of being as well as the order of the soul; the experiences of transcendence as the heart of philosophizing and the endeavors to find adequate symbolic expressions for their exegesis. The authors Voegelin dealt with in vol. V now were now examples for his own problem-oriented meditations. It is, however, revealing that in his final volume he returns to Hegel, his main philosophical adversary, as it were (nonetheless admired for his intellectual stature), and on the other hand to Hesiod, Parmenides and, above all, to Plato.

A central problem discussed in vol. V is the question how the exegesis of the experiences of existential tension in consciousness are adequately expressed in language symbols, considering the fact that words necessarily have 'object character' (*Gegenstandsförmigkeit*) and seem to refer to 'objects'. Thus, as Ellis Sandoz points out in his introduction to vol. V, there is the permanent danger of "intentionalist fallacy."[61] Voegelin contemplates this problem in the first chapter with respect to the intricacies of what it means to tell a story with a beginning and an end, and in the second chapter under the heading of "reflective distance" with the example of Plato's *Timaeus*. What Voegelin says about Plato—"Plato is struggling for a language that will optimally express the analytical movements of existential consciousness within the limits of a *fides* of the Cosmos."[62]—applies to Voegelin's own struggle to express the analytical movements of existential consciousness within the limits of "existence in the Between of thing-reality, including the bodily location of consciousness, and of Beyond-reality," and within the limits imposed by "the complex consciousness-reality-language."[63] In his epilogue to *In Search of Order* Jürgen Gebhardt stresses that for Voegelin "the recovery of experiences of reality implies the emancipation from deformed language that is dissociated from the engendering experiences," and

61 *In Search of Order*, p. 23–24.
62 Ibid., p. 108.
63 Ibid., p. 45.

that from *The Ecumenic Age* on "Voegelin had pursued this problem to the point at which the language of the questioning itself became the subject of reflection."[64]

In Search of Order was left incomplete, and thus, one could say, the whole enterprise of *Order and History*. On the other hand, it seems fitting that a volume bearing the title *In Search of Order* was not finished. This search cannot come to an end; there is no "final word," as Carl J. Friedrich had hoped for, and there is no "ultimate truth," as Voegelin stated, "that would transform the search into a possession of truth."[65] Consequently there is no final word about the order of history either. Nonetheless, it is challenging to make an attempt at an evaluation of *Order and History* "as a whole."

Voegelin's *Order and History* had its own history that could well bear the title of vol. V, *In Search of Order*, as superordinate title. What is most admirable in Voegelin, I think, is his continuous intellectual development, his never being satisfied with a particular "state of the science" already achieved, his incessant pressing forward and posing new questions, and his readiness to give up positions he regarded to be untenable, his willingness to revise his position and to try to differentiate his theoretical endeavors further and further. This characteristic of Voegelin's intellectual stature is one important bond that holds the five volumes of *Order and History* together. There are others, of course. I have delineated the "break" between the original program of *Order and History* and vol. IV, as well as the renewed changes of vol. V. Nonetheless, the five volumes do not fall apart into separate entities. In his erudite introduction to *The Ecumenic Age*, Michael Franz points out that many early reviewers have overemphasized the departures from the first three volumes, perhaps being misled by Voegelin's use of the term "break," and he rightly stresses the continuities despite the obvious revisions of the program and the more differentiated analytical approaches.[66]

That the order of history emerges from the history of order, as the first sentence of *Order and History* read, maintained its validity for the whole

---

64 Ibid., p. 130.
65 E. Voegelin, "Equivalences of Experience and Symbolization in History," *The Collected Works of Eric Voegelin*, vol. 12: *Published Essays 1966–1985*, p. 129.
66 *The Ecumenic Age*, pp. 5, 18–19.

enterprise. There was, however, a certain change in the meaning of this sentence over the years and a shift of accent. The "history of order" was no longer viewed as a continuous process of differentiation, and, consequently, the "order of history" not as a configuration that can be described from the outside, but as an open field structured by spiritual outbursts that illuminate man's perpetual search of order from the inside. "Yet the unfinished story of *Order and History* acquires an end," Jürgen Gebhardt writes in his epilogue to *In Search of Order*, referring to Voegelin's own words, "acquires an end, or *telos*, in itself at the very moment of being read by other men and women. It becomes "an event in a vast social field of thought and language, of writing and reading about matters that the members of the field believe to be of concern for their existence in truth."[67]

67 *In Search of Order*, p. 125; quotation p. 27.

Acknowledgments

The author wishes to acknowledge with gratitude permission to reprint the essays of this volume:

"The Paradox of Rhetoric," in *Sophia and Praxis. The Boundaries of Politics*. J. M. Porter, ed., Chatham, N. J.: Chatham House Publishers, Inc., 1984, p. 93–104

"Unity through *Bildung*: A German Dream of Perfection," in *Independent Journal of Philosophy*. Vol. 5/6: Modernity (2), 1988, p. 47–55.

"German Nationalism and the Concept of *Bildung*," in *Romantic Nationalism in Europe*. J. C. Eade, ed. Canberra: Australian National University, Humanities Research Centre, 1983, p. 135–150.

"Millenarianism, Hermeticism, and the Search for a Universal Science," in *Science, Pseudo-Science, and Utopianism in Early Modern Thought*. Stephen A. McKnight, ed. Columbia and London: University of Missouri Press, 1992, p. 118–140.

"Planetary Consequences: Ernst Jünger on the Meaning of the First World War," in *Tel Aviver Jahrbuch für deutsche Geschichte*, Vol. 44 (2016): *Deutsche Offiziere. Militarismus und die Akteure der Gewalt*. Galili Shahar, ed. Göttingen: Wallstein Verlag, 2016, p. 122–132

"Transhumanism: The Final Revolution," in *Revolutions: Finished and Unfinished, From Primal to Final*. Paul Caringella, Wayne Cristaudo, Glenn Hughes, eds. Newcastle upon Tyne: Cambridge Scholars Publishing, 2012, p. 364–371

"Spiritual Revolution and Magic: Speculation and Political Action in National Socialism," in *Modern Age* Vol. 23, No. 4, Fall 1979, p. 394–402

"National Socialism as a Political Religion: Potentials and Limits of an Analytical Concept," in *Totalitarian Movements and Political Religions*, vol. 6/1 (June 2005), p. 87–95

"Are Political Religions and Civil Religions Secularizations of Traditional Religions?" in *World Religions in Secular Societies in the Age of Globalization: Problems and Chances. Review of Religions*, 2016. Vol. 1. Beijing: Press of Religious Culture, 2016, p. 126–137

"Eric Voegelin, the Crisis of Western Civilization, and the Apocalypse," in *International and Interdisciplinary Perspectives on Eric Voegelin*. Stephen A. McKnight and Geoffrey L. Price, eds., Columbia and London: University of Missouri Press, 1997, p. 117–134

"Rereading Eric Voegelin's *Order and History.*" Review Article, in *International Journal of the Classical Tradition* (IJCT) 11.1. (2004), p. 80–94

Index